GW00632335

If you would like to find out more about waterways, these three books will help you. Each is available in hardback and paperback.

For general interest
INTRODUCING INLAND WATERWAYS by Charles Hadfield
Chapters: Come Canalling; Cruising on Your Own; How We Got Our Canals; Canals at Work; Keeping the Canals Open; Looking at Canals; Searching Out the Past; Meeting Others and Doing Things; Going Abroad.

For history at home and abroad
THE CANAL AGE by Charles Hadfield
Chapters: How Canals Began; They Come to Britain; They are Promoted; Where the Money Came From; Engineering and Construction; Carrying Goods; Carrying Passengers; How Canal Companies Worked; Boats and Boatmen; Aspects of the Age; To Modern Times in Britain; The Great Ship Canals; The Age on the Continent; The Age in North America.

For cruising
HOLIDAY CRUISING ON INLAND WATERWAYS by Charles Hadfield and Michael Streat
Chapters: The Pleasures of Boating; The Inland Waterways Today; Planning a Cruise; Under Way; Bridges, Tunnels and Locks; Hiring a Boat; Buying a Boat; Narrow Boats and their Conversion; Maintenance; To Help You Enjoy Your Boat.

OTHER BOOKS BY CHARLES HADFIELD

British Canals: an illustrated history
The Canal Age
The Canals of the East Midlands
The Canals of North West England (with Gordon Biddle)
The Canals of South and South East England
The Canals of South Wales and the Border
The Canals of South West England
The Canals of the West Midlands
Canals of the World
The Canals of Yorkshire and North East England
Holiday Cruising on Inland Waterways (with Michael Streat)
Introducing Inland Waterways
Waterways to Stratford (with John Norris)

WATERWAYS
SIGHTS TO SEE

CHARLES HADFIELD

with plates,
plans by
RICHARD DEAN
and text illustrations by
ROBERT COX

DAVID & CHARLES
NEWTON ABBOT LONDON
NORTH POMFRET (VT) VANCOUVER

ISBN 0 7153 7303 X
Library of Congress Catalog Card Number 76–5513

Set in 11 on 12pt Bembo
and printed in Great Britain
by Redwood Burn Limited
for David & Charles (Publishers) Limited
Brunel House Newton Abbot Devon

Published in the United States of America
by David & Charles Inc
North Pomfret Vermont 05053 USA

Published in Canada
by Douglas David & Charles Limited
1875 Welch Street North Vancouver BC

CONTENTS

PREFACE

This is a book for those who enjoy – or who think they might enjoy – inland waterways. Intended mainly for the man or woman with a car (and a pair of legs) rather than a boat, it makes suggestions for places to visit and things to see. The family can come too.

I have chosen sixty sights. Some are famous, many well known to waterway lovers, a few my own favourites, one or two a little off-beat. Some are single structures or places, in which case I have suggested other things to see in their neighbourhood. Some are short walks, or drives linking related sights. I hope that the variety will interest you.

The sights are arranged very roughly clockwise round Britain, starting from London. At the head of each section is the OS map number in the 1:50,000 series, and to make places easier to find I have given map references, which apply equally to the 1:50,000 series or to the older 1-inch. Each OS sheet carries an explanation of how map references work for those unfamiliar with these useful devices.

A section headed 'Where to Find more Information' follows the text. References to books can be followed up there.

I have written this book from enjoyment and long affection. It has taken me back to many old friends, made me discover more about them, helped me to meet new people connected with them. Maybe you will find enjoyment and affection too.

Little Venice   Charles Hadfield
February 1976

I

London: Little Venice
Map 176, ref: 262819

Venice – one pictures beautiful houses along watery streets.
Turn off the Edgware Road, come off Westway, or take the
Underground to Warwick Avenue station and you will discover
something of Venice in old Paddington.

Warwick Avenue bridge looks over water on both sides. To
the east the long line of Regent's Canal between Blomfield Road
and Maida Avenue runs dark and shining under big plane trees
to the mouth of Maida Hill tunnel. Beautiful and individual
houses of the 1830s give it a dreamy charm, and boats are moored
along the towpath. Snuggled under the bridge is a neat flat-
roofed canal house built by the canal company in 1859. This
canal, beginning here at Warwick Avenue, runs by Regent's Park
and Islington down to the Thames at Limehouse. The first
section was opened in 1816, the whole in 1820.

On the other side of the bridge Little Venice opens out into
the broad sheet of water that forms the junction between the
Regent's Canal and its predecessor, the Paddington branch of the
Grand Junction that leads by Rickmansworth and Tring (No 7)
to Stoke Bruerne (No 56), Braunston (No 55) and so to the
Midlands and beyond. To the left past the small public garden
is the line to the Grand Junction's end at Paddington Basin,
adjoining Edgware Road and Praed Street; ahead, the canal's
main line. Good houses border the wide basin to the right,
pleasant flats to the left. The green bushy island is the remaining
unexcavated part of the land at the junction: once called Rat or
Swan island, it is now Browning's island, for the poet when a
widower lived from 1862 to 1887 in a house in Warwick
Crescent, No 19 (now replaced by flats):

'that new stuccoed third house from the bridge,
Fresh painted, rather smart than otherwise!'

The bridge can be seen across the basin, on its far side the
Canal Office, one of the prettiest houses on the scene, built in 1801,

the year the Paddington branch was opened. Known as Paddington Stop, a wooden roof once spanned the narrowed section in front of it to protect cargoes and toll-collectors while boats were being gauged (their depth measured to check their cargo tonnage) beneath.

Across the road from the canal office, the water buses start for the Zoo in summertime (enquiries 01-286-6101). Further along the main line are houseboats on the right and moorings for visitors on the left. Opposite 60 Blomfield Road, the *Jason* trip-boat starts (enquiries 01-286-3428).

Little Venice is a very early example of a busy commercial canal being used as a feature of a residential estate. It epitomises my own ideas about the canal scene. Except for the Canal Office, nothing in sight dates from the early years of either canal: everything has been added, at all times up to our own. So to my mind should canal scenes change, embodying many pasts in the present for the pleasure and interest of the future.

Places Nearby

From the Canal Office a walk westwards can be taken along Delamere Terrace and then beside the canal to Harrow Road, beyond which a stretch of towpath is open partly beneath Westway, the motorway which here curves astonishingly right over the water and back again.

In the opposite direction from an entrance across Maida Vale in Lisson Grove, the towpath is open past iron-columned 'Blow-up' bridge beneath which a barge carrying gunpowder and petroleum exploded in 1874, and past the Zoo and the *Barque and Bite* floating restaurant to Camden Town. Here the Camden lock development of restaurant, little shops and workshops should be seen. The *Jenny Wren* trip-boat starts here (enquiries 01-485-6210). At Camden Town, too, is the first of the locks that carries the Regent's Canal downwards to meet the Thames. It is guarded by an exuberant crenellated lockhouse and a good iron over-bridge.

2

London: Bow Locks to Tower Bridge
Map 177, ref: 383824

I have chosen Bow locks on the river Lee (or Lea) in east London
because commercial traffic is often to be seen there and also
because here, off the hot and roaring road, is an oasis of seagull-
haunted quiet and coolness. The pair of mechanised locks stands
at the top of tidal Bow Creek; therefore get there near the top of
the tide (consult *Whitaker's Almanack*) if you want to see a tug
taking a train of lighters through, the latter helped by a power-
operated capstan. An old iron footbridge with supporting pillars
spans the locks, while north of it a modern horsebridge takes the
towpath. The island site is curiously isolated, the lock cut being
between the river and the Limehouse Cut. This was built in 1770
to give easy access to the Lee navigation from the Thames
towards the Pool of London.

To get to Bow locks, approach from the north by St Leon-
ard's Street. After passing over the railway bridge at Bromley-by-
Bow station, take the slip road ahead. Just beyond the *Rising Sun*
cross the Limehouse Cut to the towpath down to the locks and
the traffic office.

The towpath along the Limehouse Cut itself has had to be
closed. Using the street atlas, make your way therefore to
Narrow Street beside the Thames at Shadwell, either by way of
East India Dock Road or by Devons Road (if the latter, stop at
The Widow's Son). The door of *The Grapes* at 76 Narrow Street
opens onto as small and cheerful a bar as you have ever struck;
through it and the Dickens Bar beyond is a tiny balcony where
one can look down Limehouse reach to Deptford. The pub
claims to be the original of one in *Our Mutual Friend*, hence the
Dickens touch. It is all dark beams, snug, heads close together
but friendly.

Then work west along Narrow Street. On your right you will
see the filled-in entrance tide-lock of the Limehouse Cut. The
lock was closed in 1968, access to the Cut being provided by a
new channel made to it from Limehouse Basin. Just beyond, you

will pass over the entrance, built in the 1870s, to what began as Limehouse Basin, then became Regent's Canal dock and is now once again Limehouse Basin. The growth of the dock since 1820 is shown on the plan on pp232–3 of *CEM* (see Where to Find More Information). Once a busy point for transhipping narrow boat cargoes to lighters and ships, the eleven-acre basin is now little used except for lighters crossing it to reach Limehouse Cut, and awaits a new purpose.

From Narrow Street continue into The Highway, and so by Glamis Road and Wapping Wall to Wapping High Street. You will pass *The Prospect of Whitby* with its riverside verandah, then at Wapping station the top of Brunel's shaft – once carrying a spiral staircase – to the Thames tunnel, first underwater tunnel in the world; then a stretch of active riverside wharfage, lorries crowded in the street, cargo in slings above you, fork-lifts in and out at warehouses; then *The Town of Ramsgate* with an open river view from beyond the bar.

Then up towards Tower Bridge, till you must park and continue by footpath. Behind the big modern Tower Hotel is a surprising new waterside world. Some of Telford's and Hardwick's grand warehouse buildings for St Katherine dock, one of London's earliest commercial enclosed docks, have been saved and converted for modern uses – housing, business, yachting. The hotel is designed to accord with them. This to my mind is a really good development.

Between the warehouses are linked areas of water, part marina full of seagoing cruisers, part nautical museum with the steam tug *Challenge*, the old Nore lightship and several restored Thames sailing barges. Finally, work round to the front of the hotel and see against the well loved background of Tower Bridge and the upper Pool the air-and-water sculpture of the girl somersaulting over the happy dolphin – by David Wynne in 1973.

3

London: Kew Bridge to Hammersmith Bridge
Map 176, refs: 190779/230781

I have chosen this sight to take in a London riverside village, a good modern housing development that uses water in its design, and some of the capital's finest waterside streets.

Strand-on-the-Green, once a fisherman's village, borders the north side of the tidal Thames just east of Kew Bridge. I walked down from the bridge in early spring to a footpath that leads between the river and the jumbled houses. The long Oliver's or Strand Ait (island) parallels the path, with boat moorings above and below, and seagulls floating backwards on the ebb. Trees line the path. Behind, there are steps up to each house in case of floods. Some have balconies, some creepers, some both. Jessamine and daffodils are out; cotoneaster, laurustinus and Whitsuntide bosses; and a promise of wisteria. Walk a few yards up Post Office Alley (postmen must have been short in those days), then back to the *City Barge*, so called because the City Corporation from 1777 moored barges here, first to collect river tolls until a bankside tollhouse was built, then for the Lord Mayor to use. Beyond the pub, trains rumble over the right sort of iron bridge to interest the eye: one can study it well from outside the *Bull's Head* or from the row of four almshouses dated 1704.

Strand-on-the-Green is crowded in summer, but in spring, autumn, or, indeed, winter, it is London refreshment.

Follow the path to Grove Road, fork right into Hartington Road for Chiswick Quay. Cubitt's Yacht Basin used to be here, a large irregular patch of water linked with the river and full of jumbled houseboats. Now the old basin is surrounded on three sides by new terrace houses. Varying roof heights, clever use of land levels and the enclosed water make as nice a modern development as one could ask for. After Chiswick Quay, if you are walking, cross Great Chertsey Road and turn right. You will soon come to the riverside path through Duke's Meadows, past Barnes Bridge to Chiswick Mall. By car, turn left into Great Chertsey Road and make for Church Street, Chiswick, and the Mall.

Charming, higgledy-piggledy Church Street runs down to the river. The church has a canal link: a memorial (opposite the door) to Thomas Bentley who helped Josiah Wedgwood promote the Trent & Mersey Canal. At the street's end, if the tide is out, you can walk down the draw-dock to look past the nearby house-boats to the end of Chiswick Eyot (island), or sit to watch the tugs, cruisers, scullers and eights go by.

Chiswick Mall begins here: its seventeenth- and eighteenth-century houses look across the road to their gardens, willows and the water. At the far end it becomes smaller, more intimate, with houses now on both sides shutting out the water until, past Hammersmith Terrace where A.P. Herbert once lived, the new Furnivall Gardens open out the river once more, Hammersmith Bridge now in sight. The Gardens are where Hammersmith Creek once was – a short canal branch of the river where sailing barges and narrow boats unloaded. On the far side is the *Old Ship*.

On past a sailing club's pontoons and crow's nest judges' box to delightful Upper Mall, Hammersmith, with the *Dove* in a footway beyond. On the balcony with its vine you may listen to the seagulls' male voice choir on Hammersmith pier. Beyond, a pathway leads along Lower Mall to the great suspension bridge, past houseboats, cruiser moorings and beginners learning to row in clinker fours. No ironwork was ever so ornamental as that on its towers and over its chain anchors. Further along, on the same side, a stretch of industrial Thameside, barge tiers and all, offers an increasingly rare sight.

4

Brentford
Map 176, refs: 190779/174774

Brentford is a good place to see barges working. Choose a time of day when the tide is up (tide tables in *Whitaker's Almanack*).

Start at Kew Bridge. Nearby you will see the fine 190ft-high Victorian waterworks tower. In 1811, the Grand Junction Canal

Co set up a separate water company. In 1838 the intake was moved here from Chelsea and, earlier, Little Venice. When an 1852 Act prohibited water being taken from below Teddington lock, Kew Bridge became a filtration and pumping station. The Grand Junction Water Works Co ceased to exist in 1904, but the works remain. Inside are five beam engines, including a Boulton & Watt of 1820 and the only Maudslay in existence. A trust preserves the engines and steams them; they can be visited at weekends.

On the west side of Kew Bridge, walk down to the river and then turn upstream to follow a path past willows and moored houseboats – some former sailing barges among them – to Brentford High Street. Follow this past the Piano Museum (in a church) to Ferry Lane on the left. Here is the *Watermans Arms* and, by the wharf, a multi-purpose sandstone pillar economically commemorating Cassivelaunus opposing Julius Caesar at the Thames ford here in 54BC, a church council held by King Offa in 780–1, and the battle of Brentford in 1642.

Then back to High Street, and to the left again at Dock Road (opposite St Paul's Road) to reach Thames locks, the tidal pair that connect the Grand Union Canal to the river. There used to be one; the second was built in 1962. They have power-operated gates and fascinating power capstans that fire barges out of the lock and up the cut. Across the canal, a housing estate stands on what was Brentford railway dock. Part is kept as pleasure craft moorings.

Then walk along the lockside furthest from the lockhouse, and take a path past the remains of Dr Johnson's lock (it gave access to the canal from a tidal creek) and the *Brewery Tap* (ship prints and a telegraph at Full Ahead on the bar) to Catherine Wheel Road and High Street. Turn left, then right along the right-hand side of the magistrate's court into The Butts with its old houses. On the left is the Boatmen's Institute, built in 1904 behind Brentford canal depot. Such mission buildings were once common.

A little further west along High Street is the 1824 bridge over the canalised Brent. To the right, the towpath runs beside the mechanised pair of Brentford locks. Narrow boats were once gauged here: that is, the weight of cargo carried was discovered by rods which indicated the depth at which the boat was floating. The depth at various loads having been previously measured, the cargo and so the toll to be charged were at once known. The warehouses of the modern depot, functional and pleasant, are opposite and beyond – the towpath runs through one of them.

Brentford is an export barge groupage depot, with 150,000 sq ft of covered and 50,000 sq ft of open storage, nine covered and eight open barge berths and efficient handling equipment. Goods arrive by road or water to be grouped by the ship in which they are to travel. Then Thames lighters take them to the docks to be loaded direct. The Greater London Council and the British Waterways Board are now considering whether to enlarge the lower few miles of the canal to a point near the M1 and M4, where a road/water transhipment centre could be built. Thus heavy lorries would not need to pass through London streets to reach the docks.

5

Rye and the Royal Military Canal
Map 189

Fear of invasion by Napoleon was as real to our ancestors as of invasion by Hitler was to our fathers or ourselves. That neither happened is no criticism of the precautions taken. The Royal Military Canal was one of them: a defence work 30 miles long built between 1804 and 1806 incorporating drainage ditches, canal, parapet and military road, aimed at 'separating an Enemy landed upon the Coast of Romney Marsh from the Interior of the Country'. The line began at the sea at Shorncliffe beyond Hythe and ran round the Marsh to the Rother at Iden, then incorporated the Rother to its junction with the Brede at Rye, ran along the Brede to Strand bridge near Winchelsea, and thence by a smaller canal to its terminus at Cliff End. These three rivers were then all navigable by small sailing craft; today, cruisers may explore the Brede to Brede village, or the Rother to Bodiam.

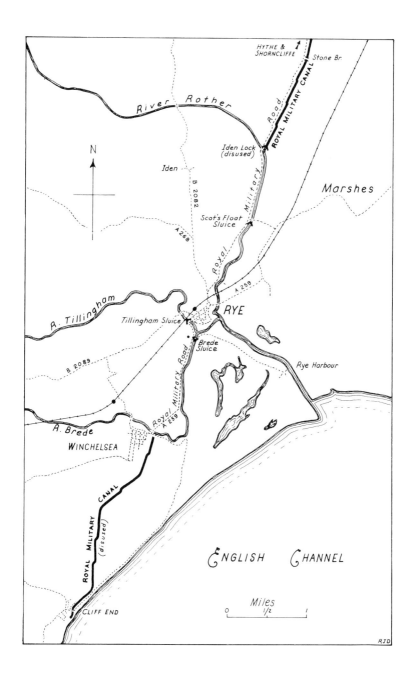

The western sections of the defence line round picturesque Rye with its cobbled streets make an unusual sight to see. Begin, I suggest, at ref: 919198, where the Rye Harbour road leaves the Military Road running towards Winchelsea and crosses the Brede. Under the bridge is Brede Sluice, a small navigation lock with two pairs of upper gates facing opposite ways, the inner pair acting as floodgates against a tide higher than the river. Nearby is a Martello tower, one of the squat circular forts that were also part of the coast defences. Down the road is Rye Harbour, part fishing village, boats lining the tidal channel, part busy small port, its modern wharf sheds showing prosperity.

From Brede Sluice follow the Military Road as it loops back over the Tillingham. Here is Tillingham Sluice, a vertical gate that can either keep a high tide out or release flood water at low tide. A grey weatherboarded windmill, rows of yachts and old boarded warehouses mark the Quay. Follow this road round Rye, parking perhaps by the foundry to walk up Gun Garden Steps to the *Ypres Castle* below the medieval Ypres tower and with easy access on foot to the oldest part of the town.

Then on to join the A268, to fork right past the railway to the Military Road. On the right at ref: 933227 is Scot's Float Sluice, the Rother's only navigation lock. Beyond, at ref. 936245, is disused Iden lock, where the Royal Military Canal joined the Rother. The plan on p170 of Mr Vine's book shows the old layout. The officers' quarters of the military still stand beside the lock, the barracks across the road. The porched annexe nearest the road was used as a tollhouse when charges were made to pass the Military Road.

Further on is Stone (or Knock) bridge at ref: 946266. On your way notice occasional zigzags of the road. They mark similar zigzags of the canal, built thus so that guns could fire down each stretch without hitting the defenders of neighbouring stretches. At Stone bridge the construction of the defence work can easily be seen: back drain, military road, parapet, canal, towing path and front drain – 168ft wide in all.

Places Nearby
Hythe is near the other end of the canal. Rowboats and canoes

can be hired there for a potter along the canal's tree-shaded length.

Every other year (even dates) Hythe has a Venetian Fête. It is, I suppose, the oldest canal event in England, for it was first held in 1860. The fête itself is the end of an August week of jollification: the mayor has a barge, the Queen of the Fête has another, there is a daylight parade of floating tableaux, waterborne musicmakers, a grand display of aquatic fireworks, and a final parade of illuminated tableaux. If you should miss the Fête, there is still the Romney, Hythe & Dymchurch Railway, with its terminal station at Hythe alongside the canal. This 15in-gauge line using miniature steam locomotives runs all the year round (enquiries New Romney 2353).

6

Guildford to Godalming
Map 186, refs: 995494/975440

Here is an opportunity to explore four miles of pretty Surrey river, preferably in a day's row, and to see what one town has made of its river front and what some volunteers are doing on an ambitious canal restoration project.

High Street, Guildford – one of England's most attractive streets – runs down to its bridge over the river. The Wey was made navigable from the Thames at Weybridge to here in 1653, and in 1763 on to Godalming. In 1958 Guildford saw its last working barge, and between 1963 and 1969 the navigation was transferred to the National Trust by its last owner, Harry Stevens.

There is a car park at Millbrook a little way down the A281. I suggest a walk back towards the town past Debenham's to the 200-year-old treadmill crane that once stood on Guildford wharf beside Harry Stevens's office. Until 1908 it was worked by a man walking the 18ft diameter wheel. There are others in England, but to my knowledge this is the only one on a waterway. Nostalgically, I regret the disappearance of Mr Stevens's little wharf office with its high desk and dusty papers on rows of spikes, but just as that typified one period of the waterway, the present river front typifies another.

Then back past Debenham's (which has a riverside restaurant) and the town mill that dates from 1766, and round the curved glass front of the Yvonne Arnaud theatre, its restaurant and foyer making good use of their riverside position. A footpath leads on to Mill Mead lock (ref: 996492). Locks are found at intervals on canalised rivers like the Wey, each on a short side-cut and parallelled by a weir of the same height. From this tree-shaded open space a short walk up the towpath shows us a boathouse and the *Jolly Farmer* across the water. Trip-boats start from the former (enquiries Guildford 4494) or one can hire a rowing boat. Access to both is from beside Millbrook car park. From here one can walk the four-mile towpath past St Catherine's lock ($1\frac{1}{8}$ miles from Mill Mead), Unstead lock ($2\frac{3}{8}$ miles) and Catteshall lock ($3\frac{5}{8}$ miles), to Godalming, a stretch that includes some of the river's loveliest scenery.

On our way, let us pause $\frac{3}{4}$ mile above St Catherine's lock, for here, on the left, is the entrance to the Wey & Arun Junction Canal. Opened in 1816, $18\frac{1}{2}$ miles long with 23 locks, it joined the canalised Arun at Newbridge above Pallingham. By the Arun Littlehampton could be reached, or Portsmouth through another then existing canal, the Portsmouth & Arundel (now also a target for restoration) to Chichester harbour. The Wey & Arun was abandoned in 1871, but now the Wey & Arun Canal Trust has begun energetically to restore it, so that once again boats may pass from the Wey to the south coast by London's lost route to the sea. From the A281 at ref: 997464 the canal can be seen close to its junction with the Wey (a brick parapet marks the spot), its banks lined with moored craft.

For those who would like to visit a section that has been dredged after a hundred years of disuse, there is a mile at Run Common (ref: 033419), with a walk down a shady length of towpath. Or drive to Newbridge at the other end of the canal (map 187, ref: 068260) where an 1837 warehouse built by the Arun navigation still stands beside its silted basin, and follow the restored canal back along the towpath to Rowner's lock, the first upwards from the Arun.

Continuing up the Wey past Unstead, we come to Catteshall lock among fields and woods at ref: 981444, accessible from the A3100. Here at Farncombe boathouse one may hire a skiff or punt, join a trip-boat (enquiries Godalming 21306), or sit out by the café. Half a mile above the lock on a sharp curve are pleasant moorings facing open country at Godalming wharf, from which the town is easily reached.

7

Tring Reservoirs
Map 165

The canal at Tring offers a nature reserve with good walking and an unusual variety of canal buildings at the lock flights, junctions and yards.

The Grand Union climbing from London by lock after broad lock up the Chilterns past Berkhamsted reaches its summit level at nearly 400ft at Cowroast lock (ref: 958104) where the lock-keeper has a small museum, and then enters peacefully wooded Tring cutting. At its far end beside the B488 is Bulbourne maintenance yard, a pleasant group of Victorian slated brick buildings, one with a nice ornamental tower. Here, among other work, about fourteen pairs of lock gates a year are made to measure by hand – for no two locks are just the same size. After visiting the nearby *Lock and Quay*, we can walk on down the towpath to where, at Bulbourne junction, the former Wendover branch runs to the left. It leaked badly and is now watered only to Tringford pumping station, though the towpath offers a pleasant country walk to Wendover.

As a boat works upwards to the summit of such a canal as the Grand Union, it draws off some 56,000 gallons to fill the last lock – in this case Cowroast. As it leaves the other end of the summit, Marsworth top lock, it takes another 56,000 gallons with it. Therefore, since 1802 a network of reservoirs, inter-

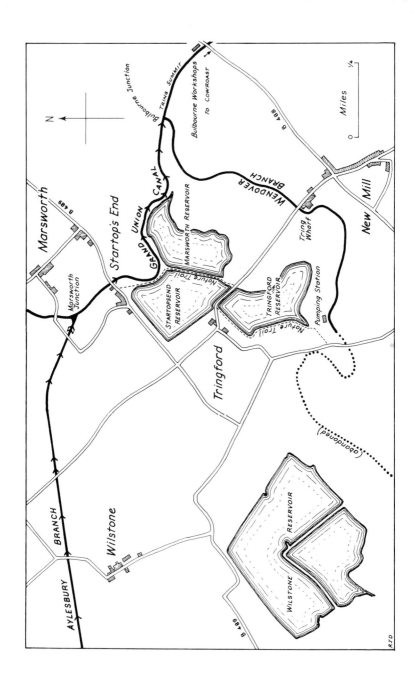

connected by pumping stations, has been built here; how it grew is shown on the plan on p182 of Mr Faulkner's book. Today all pumping is concentrated at Tringford. The reservoirs, all beneath canal summit level, are connected by underground culverts to Tringford which pumps water as required up into the Wendover branch, whence it feeds the canal.

The reservoirs are a national nature reserve. Flocks of wintering wildfowl come here and many varieties breed. Herons nest in the reed-beds, sea-birds visit it, and migrants come in spring and autumn. There are of course insects and plants and many kinds of animal – though the edible dormouse, understandably, may be too shy to show himself. A leaflet with much information and a footpath map may be obtained from the Nature Conservancy Council (enquiries 0233-812525). A nature trail runs from a little south west of the bridge at Startops End (ref: 920142) along the edge of Startopsend reservoir, back parallel to the canal, then across the embankment between it and Marsworth reservoirs, and left round Tringford reservoir to the pumping station and the Wendover branch towpath.

Beyond Bulbourne junction on the main line with its imposing canal house and covered dry-dock, the canal drops from the summit through seven Marsworth locks. These have side-ponds to economise on water, ie, water from an emptying lock can be run into them, and then back, partly to fill it next time. The double-arched bridge at the foot of the flight reminds us that there was great waste of water in the early days of the canal by single narrow boats using the broad locks. Therefore in 1838–9 narrow locks were built alongside. Later, as water supplies improved and engined boats tended to move in pairs, these narrow locks were filled in. Some can be traced.

A branch runs to the left from Marsworth Junction beside the piling workshops. Opened in 1815 ten years after the main line's completion, it falls by sixteen narrow locks, the first two a staircase pair (ie sharing a common centre gate) for $6\frac{1}{4}$ miles to Aylesbury Basin. The main line, falling also, winds on past Cheddington and Ivinghoe on its way to Leighton Buzzard.

'Bulbourne maintenance yard, a pleasant group of Victorian slated brick buildings, one with a nice ornamental tower'

Places Nearby
Maybe drive through Aldbury to the soaring Doric column (ref: 970131) surmounted by an urn put up in 1832 at Ashridge, that commemorates the third (canal) Duke of Bridgewater whose property Ashridge had been. Then, if you are driving back to London on the A41, take the lane to the left at Winkwell for a visit to the *Three Horseshoes* spreading prettily beside the canal or, by the second turning to the left further on, relax at the *Fishery* inn at Boxmoor.

8

Abingdon
Map 164

A lovely little Thames-side town; reminders of the Wilts & Berks Canal, a power-operated Thames lock and the oldest surviving lock chamber in Britain. Enough for a good day out.

Abingdon lies some six miles from Oxford by road and eight by river. Sited on one bank, it looks across the Thames to open country. Begin, I suggest, in Market Place and walk down East St Helen Street, as beautiful an old street as one could find. Then left past the church to St Helen's wharf and the *Old Anchor* facing the river. Just beyond, the river Ock enters the Thames under an iron bridge. The river side of the arch is inscribed: 'Erected by the Wilts and Berks Canal Company A.D. 1824'. This canal, narrow-locked, ran for fifty-one miles from here past Wantage, Swindon and Melksham to the Kennet & Avon at Semington above Bradford-on-Avon. It was opened throughout on 22 September 1810, when shareholders 'in the Company's boat, with music playing and colours flying, passed the last lock into the river Thames amidst the loud huzzas of the multitude'. Overwhelmed by railway competition, it was abandoned in 1914.

Over the stream, turn left into Wilsham Road. Here the Hygienic Laundry occupies a warehouse. The canal came in from the right past the far wall of the building, and joined the river on the left of the road, where original stonework can be seen. Just beyond, on the right, part of the canal wharf entrance remains. The wharf walls now enclose a small housing estate, Wharf Close. Inside this the first house on the left is the wharfinger's, a good stone building with a pedimented centre and two wings. Wharf Cottage, which probably once housed the lockkeeper, is in Wilsham Road beyond Wharf Close. Then walk back along Wilsham Road and turn into Caldecott Road. Beyond the laundry the road opens out with a wide grassy space to the left: this is the line of the Wilts & Berks coming in from Wantage way, the far hedge being that of the canal.

Round to the left, the back wall of the wharf can be seen enclosing the Wharf Close houses.

Back now to Market Place, and down Bridge Street. Cross both the backwater and the main river by the bridge, originally built in 1416–17, then down to the towpath and upstream to Abingdon lock (ref: 506971). The original navigation channel, as we shall see, ran through Swift Ditch or Back Water and by-passed Abingdon, to which goods were brought by road from Culham. In 1788 local businessmen persuaded the Thames Commissioners to alter Abingdon bridge to take barges and build a lock. Swift Ditch then ceased to be used. Today the modern lock with its power-operated gates is busy with pleasure craft, a picturesque spot beside its neat lockhouse and rushing sluices.

If you now continue along the buttercup-bordered towpath to a gate, then walk half-right along a path over the meadow, you will come first to one bridge over a backwater, then to a second. Unbelievably, the main stream of the Thames once ran here. Just upstream of the second bridge is a ruined lock chamber of masonry patched with brick and timber, one gate recess still visible (ref: 513966). This oldest of extant British locks was built between 1624 and 1635 by the Oxford-Burcot Commission, the Thames' first navigation authority (Burcot is below Clifton Hampden). It was used until Abingdon lock replaced it in 1790. Let all lovers of inland waterways salute it.

One can return to the town by crossing the tail-gates of Abingdon lock and taking the path over the sluices and beside the millstream. The tall spire of St Helen's church parallels the poplars as one approaches by way of a riverside recreation ground and the old abbey gateway.

9

Crofton Pumping Station
Map 174, ref: 262623

There is not, I hope, a man or boy in Britain who has not learned

that James Watt first realised the power of steam while watching his mother's kettle, or cannot recognise the name of Boulton & Watt, the firm that resulted from his partnership with the Birmingham businessman Matthew Boulton. At Crofton, on the Kennet & Avon Canal, you can see the only Boulton & Watt engine that is still doing the work for which it was originally installed. Built in 1812 while James Watt was still alive, it is the oldest working steam engine in the world.

Crofton pumping station, begun in 1800, was intended to supply the summit level of the Kennet & Avon barge canal between Crofton top lock and the first of the four falling Wootton Rivers locks. The brick-built enginehouse, with its separated iron-bound chimney, stands high above the canal near Great Bedwyn not far from Hungerford.

The first Boulton & Watt engine installed here began work in 1809. A second was ordered in 1812, the one we still have. Both were low-pressure engines working at $4\frac{1}{2}$psi, fitted with Watt's parallel motion linkage and his patent separate condenser. In 1844 the 1812 engine was converted to a higher working pressure of 20psi by Harvey's of Hayle, and a Sims engine was installed to replace that of 1809. This had to be rebuilt in 1905 when both engines were given their present Lancashire boilers, made by the Great Western Railway (then the canal's owners) at Swindon.

The Sims engine worked till 1952, the 1812 one till 1958. In that year 20ft had to be taken off the chimney, reported unsafe. This, however, spoiled the steaming powers of the engines and the old steam-driven pumps were therefore replaced by electric ones. In 1968, Crofton was leased from the British Waterways Board by the Kennet & Avon Canal Trust who, working with the Board, are active in restoring navigation along this lovely waterway. Money was raised, volunteers got to work, and in 1970 the 1812 engine was once again in steam, pumping a ton of water at each stroke, its great beam – most thrilling of all symbols of power – pivoting across the massive dividing wall of the pumphouse, one end attached to the engine piston, the other to the pump bucket. The water raised runs along a feeder westwards, parallel to the canal, until it enters above Crofton top lock. The second engine was restored in 1971.

The pumping station is usually open to the public on Sundays, and on certain days the steam engines are worked. Enquiries Burbage 575. The steamboat *Leviathan* also offers passenger trips.

Places Nearby

Not far westwards along the canal is Bruce tunnel at Savernake, 502yds long, its cross-section surprisingly large. Boats were hauled through by the crew pulling on chains fastened to the walls. It can best be seen by getting to the towpath at Wolfhall bridge (ref: 244625) near Wilton village, and then walking towards it. There is a long inscription over the eastern entrance. Bruce tunnel takes the canal under the Western Region London–Plymouth main line. We can walk up the gentle horsepath, cross the main road by the Savernake Forest Hotel to its continuation the other side, and then pass by a tiny foot tunnel under the railway down to the western portal. All round spreads Savernake Forest, ideal for walks and picnics.

Beyond, Burbage wharf (ref: 224635) still has its wooden crane and some pleasant red-brick wharf buildings, now con-

verted. And so, perhaps, to Wootton Rivers by lock 51, delightful in itself, exceptional in its very odd church clock made
locally out of odds-and-ends to celebrate George V's coronation,
and with the words GLORY BE TO GOD used in place of
numbers on the dial.

IO

Kennet & Avon Canal: Bradford to Bath
Maps 173, 172

It is not possible to choose just one sight along the ten miles of the
Kennet & Avon Canal that wind down the valley of the Bristol
Avon from Bradford-on-Avon to Bath. There are too many.
This great barge canal was opened in 1810 to give Bristol direct
inland waterway connection with London. It had long been
unnavigable when in the mid-1960s the Kennet & Avon Canal
Trust and the British Waterways Board jointly began restoration.

Let us begin at lovely Bradford. The canal wharf (boat trip
enquiries Bradford 2129) still with dry-dock and restored buildings, lies on the B3109 at ref: 826602, by lock 14. The *Barge Inn*
neighbours it, with the *Canal Tavern* across the road. Some one
and a half miles westwards the canal swings across the Avon on
Rennie's three-arched aqueduct, completed in 1798 at Avoncliff
(ref: 804601). Stone-built in classical style, its centre sags a
little – seemingly it has always done so. The aqueduct is so
superbly placed that, as a sight, I prefer it to the architecturally
greater Dundas – and it has the attraction thrown in of the little
Crossed Guns tucked into the hillside below.

The canal now hangs to the hillside, woods above and Avon
below, till past Limpley Stoke it crosses the Avon again at
Dundas aqueduct (ref: 785626). Again the design is classical. A
wide central arch over the river is separated from narrow ones on
each side by decorative double pilasters; beyond the side arches
single pillars introduce the curving sweep of the wing-walls. As
at Avoncliff, the parapet is solid in the centre, balustraded at each
end. But here there is a wide and heavy corbelled cornice,

reminiscent of the Lune aqueduct (No 37).

Across Dundas, the canal turns north towards Bath. Formerly, an alternative turn to the south under a bridge, now gone, would have brought a narrow boat into the first lock of the Somersetshire Coal Canal, last used in 1898. The lockkeeper's is now a private house, the lock outlined in the rose garden. Just beyond on the main line is a wharf and crane, where a path runs up to the road.

A mile beyond is Claverton, a waterwheel-powered pumping plant (ref: 792643). Access is down Ferry Lane from Claverton village (enquiries Beckington 294). The enormously wide-looking waterwheel – in fact, two wheels each 11ft 6in wide on one axle – has a diameter of 15ft 6in. The wheel worked from 1813 to 1952, taking water from a leat off the Avon and raising it 53ft to the canal. Restoration, begun in 1969, is now complete.

And so to Bath. The canal curves high along the hillside through Bathampton with its canalside pub, the *George* (where its towpath can be reached for a walk into the city), into as fine a stretch of urban canal as anywhere in Britain. Views of Georgian terraces open out, until the waterway sinks into a cutting hung with houses. A short tunnel runs under Beckford Road, its inner portal decorated with a man's head set in a swag. The canal now passes through Sydney Gardens, giving us glimpses of shrubs and trees, and under two cast-iron footbridges dated 1800 and made by Stothert's of Bath. A second tunnel under Sydney Road approaches, its façade ornamented with rusticated masonry and a carved central swag. Above stands the fine classical Cleveland House, once the canal company's offices.

Through the tunnel and over a roving bridge as the towpath changes sides, and Bath curves open before us as we approach the Widcombe flight of locks (ref: 758647) down to the Avon, the top one crossed by a charmingly delicate white-painted iron footbridge. Beside it is a pleasant lock cottage (boat trip enquiries, Bath 62831). There used to be seven locks, but a new road has caused two to be amalgamated to give one with over 19ft of fall, the deepest on a British cruising waterway. Half way down the flight is an ornamental stone chimney, a relic of a canal pumping station. An enginehouse is by the bottom lock, whence the Avon navigation runs to Bristol and the sea.

II

The Grand Western Canal
Map 181

The eleven surviving miles of the Grand Western are an oddity; a barge canal the size of the Leeds & Liverpool in the heart of agricultural Devon. The western part, from Tiverton to Rock bridge, Halberton, is especially interesting for the scale of its works.

Begin at Tiverton wharf (ref: 963123), reached by turning off the A373 at a roundabout as you enter Tiverton – the canal is signposted. You come in beside the steep walls of the canal basin, limekilns built into them. Here ended the Tiverton branch of what was planned as a canal from the Exe at Topsham via Cullompton and Burlescombe to Taunton and the navigable river Tone. The branch, and a short section of the main line, were built to Lowdwells on the Somerset border in 1810–14. An extension to Taunton was made in 1831–8, which included seven vertical lifts and an inclined plane. The extension became disused in 1867; the original portion now belongs to the Devon County Council.

A horse-drawn boat, *Tivertonian*, runs trips from Tiverton in the summer (enquiries Tiverton 3345) and rowing boats and canoes can be hired. Or why not walk the towpath for five miles to Rock bridge and take a bus (infrequent, however) back? If you are driving, I suggest going first to Halberton aqueduct (ref: 997123) built in 1847, where the former Tiverton branch of the Great Western Railway passed under the canal. Viewed from below, it is a brick structure with two narrow and high arches shaped for trains. But from the towpath one sees that an iron trough holds the water.

Then on to Lower Town, Halberton, where you can park the car and walk to Change Path bridge (ref: 997127) and so along the towpath, under the A373, past a road depot to which the last barges brought stone in the 1920s, and round a great loop of canal. This lovely walk takes you above Halberton past Greenway bridge (ref: 008132), through a cutting, and out to a 50ft-high embankment before reaching Halberton wharf on the opposite bank with its modernised cottage. Beyond lies Rock bridge in red sandstone. From here you can either walk back by road to Lower Town and your car, or retrace your steps to Greenway bridge, and so to the village.

Places Nearby

Drive to Fossend bridge (ref: 069171) on the road from Burlescombe to Westleigh. Then, I suggest, walk rather over a mile to the present end of the canal, past Waytown (Beacon Hill) tunnel under the Holcombe road (boats were pulled through by men hauling on a fixed chain) to Wharf House, where are the remains of a 54ft-long lock (to take four tub-boats) with a $3\frac{1}{2}$ft fall.

If you have time, visit Nynehead also. At ref: 146220, the Taunton extension crossed the road at Nynehead wharf; the cottage is still there. Follow a path to the west, and you will find the remains of Nynehead vertical lift (24ft rise) at ref: 144218. These lifts had two counterbalanced iron tanks suspended from overhead pulleys, rising and falling within a masonry framework. A fair amount of masonry remains at Nynehead, which should be studied with the drawings in Mrs Harris's book in hand. A little way along the canal embankment above the lift, the canal crosses the former drive to Nynehead Court on an iron trough enclosed in a one-arched aqueduct of pleasant classical design. Then back to the road, and along a path the opposite way to the single-arched aqueduct over the river Tone; a plain iron trough.

12

The Exeter Canal
Map 192

The five miles of the Exeter Ship Canal from Exeter itself to the estuary of the Exe at Turf have everything, from a medieval wicked countess to Europe's finest collection of boats.

Isabella de Fortibus, the wicked Countess of Devon, so the story goes, built a weir across the Exe (the site is still called Countess Wear) to prevent boats reaching Exeter. They would therefore have to be unloaded at Topsham, where dues were payable to the Earls of Devon. The citizens of Exeter again and again took legal proceedings: sometimes the Earls obeyed orders, sometimes not. So in the end the persistent Corporation got an Act, under the powers of which in 1563 they employed John Trew as engineer, to build a little canal only 16ft wide and 3ft deep from Matford Brook below Countess Wear to Exeter. Opened in 1566, it was the first canal for navigation only ever to be built in England. It also had our first locks, which suggests that John Trew knew of those already built in Italy and Flanders. A remarkable man – and we know almost nothing about him. That little canal was extended and rebuilt more than once before the present small ship canal was opened in 1827, the basin at Exeter three years later.

Exeter quays (ref: 923919) lie beside the Exe beneath a great red sandstone cliff. At the city end is the delightful brick-built Custom House that dates from 1683. Part of the Exeter Maritime Museum is in the first of the five-storeyed warehouses on the quay; the rest is across the river (there is a manually operated ferry-boat, as there has been for 400 years) beside, and afloat in, the canal basin. The museum, open all the year, has boats from near and far ranging from a Bude Canal tub-boat fitted with wheels to run on the inclined planes or a River Fal oyster boat to a Fijian proa or a reed-boat from legendary Lake Titicaca in Bolivia. Moreover, you can hire a rowing boat there, or take a motor-boat trip down the canal to Double Locks (museum enquiries Exeter 58075).

Beyond the river quay is Trew's weir which, by holding the level up at this point, gave John Trew the water he wanted to supply his canal. It still supplies ours. Across the river is the canal entrance, guarded by the single gates of King's Arms sluice, used to give access to the river quays before the basin was built.

Rather over a mile down the towpath is Double Locks (ref: 932901) in fact one very large single lock 312ft long which enabled craft to pass each other. It must be the biggest manually-operated canal lock in the country – the bottom gates have three paddles each. What could be England's oldest pub built in connection with a canal stands beside the lock, the charming brick-built *Double Locks Inn* dating from about 1701, its tall chimneys, one at each corner, and pitched roof gazing placidly over the water.

Further on, at Countess Wear, the towpath passes a new power-operated lifting bridge of traditional canal design, and then the swing bridge carrying the Exeter by-pass. Beyond is Topsham side-lock connecting the canal with the Exe here, whence a ferry runs to the *Passage Inn* at Topsham. If you explore that pleasant riverside place, I hope the museum with its maritime interest is open for you.

And so to the canal's end at Turf (ref: 963861) where a lock, built with difficulty on piles driven through clay and bog to the rock below, gives access to the tideway of the Exe. The landlord of the *Turf Hotel*, a building perched solitary above the estuary that spreads wide between the red Devon hills down to Exmouth and the sea, doubles the duties of lockkeeper and publican. Lock and hotel can be reached by a lane from below Exminster. There or at Starcross, should you wish to continue down the Exe by way of the river wall, you can get transport back to Exeter.

13

Morwellham Quay
Map 201, ref: 445696

Morwellham, on the Devon side of the Tamar, had been

Tavistock's port in medieval times. Early in the Napoleonic wars 200-ton craft were sailing to it to take away copper ore coming from local mines. To carry the increasing output due to wartime demand, a canal was authorised in 1803. This took tub-boats 30ft × 4½ft × 2½ft holding about 4½tons from Tavistock, where it drew water from the Tavy, past Crowndale (Francis Drake's birthplace, where a mine was now opened) and on an aqueduct over the Lumburn to dive under Morwelldown in a 2,540yd tunnel, with the smallest cross-section of any in Britain, to end above Morwellham. Part was brick-arched, part rock-cut. Cargoes were then transhipped by crane to trucks running on an inclined plane with a vertical fall of 237ft and powered by a 28ft-diameter waterwheel, to be carried down to the quay below.

The canal was opened in 1817, so long had cutting the tunnel taken at about a foot a day. A branch to Mill Hill slate quarries was added by 1819. The waterway started to decline in the late 1830s, but not Morwellham Quay which, thanks to the discovery in 1844 of the Devon Great Consols group of mines, reached its peak in the 1860s. The mines were served by a mineral railway to above Morwellham, and an inclined plane down to the port. There a new dock was built, and tiled quay floors laid for ores awaiting shipment. It was all so exciting that in 1856 Queen Victoria and her family came up the Tamar by steamer to see it. Then the place became a tourist attraction, an object of Plymouth trippers' outings.

The Tavistock Canal probably closed about 1875, the quay in the 1890s, Devon Great Consols in 1901. Derelict and overgrown, Morwellham has now been restored as a centre for the study of local industrial archaeology. Useful leaflets enable visitors to explore; there is also a small museum.

This lovely spot among the wooded Tamar hills can be reached by road from Tavistock or Gunnislake, or by boat trip from Plymouth (enquiries Millbrook 202). Wharf cottages, limekilns, ore chutes, two docks and a river wharf can be seen at river level. Above, one can find the site of the inclined plane, its pit and housing at the top alongside Incline Cottage, the first section of canal, and the southern entrance to the tunnel. This was built with a slight current to help downcoming boats, those going upwards being poled through. Our ancestors were great men and women, for over 300 guests and a band went through this claustrophobic hole on the opening day. In 1933 a new cut was made near the tunnel entrance, along which the water was diverted to a hydro-electric power station. This has an information room.

Places Nearby
I suggest you visit the former canal wharf in Tavistock, still with its warehouses and feeder from the Tavy. Then walk down the towpath past Crowndale to the single-arched masonry Lumburn aqueduct, beyond which is the northern entrance to the tunnel with '1803' over its tiny portal. Between the aqueduct and the tunnel the Mill Hill branch went off. The canal bed (a horse tramroad was later built on the site and has also left remains) can be followed along the contour to Mill Hill, where there is a canal road bridge (ref: 453722).

At Cotehele (ref: 423680) across the Tamar, the National Maritime Museum is creating a gallery in a National Trust building on the quay to which Tamar sailing barges once worked. There are displays on the part the Tamar played in nineteenth-century social and industrial life, on the river's salmon fishery, and on the history of *Shamrock*, ketch-rigged, 58ft long, the last Tamar barge. Built in 1899, she continued to trade until the 1960s. Later, she was restored at Cotehele and is now moored at the quay.

14

Sharpness Docks
Map 162, ref: 673023

Industrial archaeology, canal history and a flourishing, intimate riverside port can all be enjoyed at Sharpness, plus stunning views up and down the Severn.

The Gloucester & Sharpness Canal runs from here to Glouces-

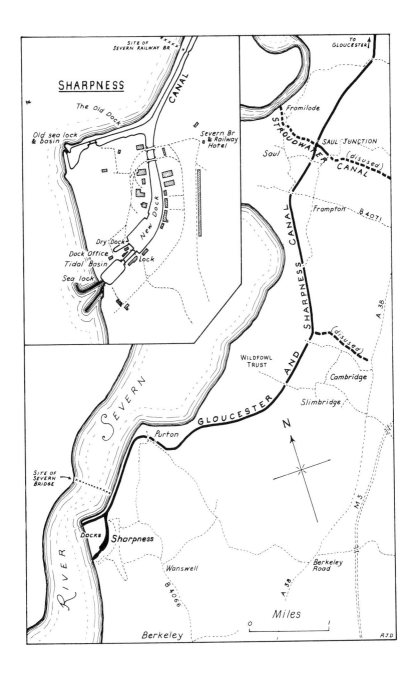

SHARPNESS

SITE OF
SEVERN RAILWAY BR

CANAL

The Old Dock

Old sea lock
& basin

Severn Br
& Railway
Hotel

Dry Dock

New Dock

Dock Office
Tidal Basin
Sea lock

Lock

TO
GLOUCESTER

Framilode

STROUDWATER

SAUL JUNCTION

Soul

(disused)

CANAL

Frampton

B 4071

SHARPNESS

AND

CANAL

(disused)

A 38

WILDFOWL
TRUST

Cambridge

Slimbridge

GLOUCESTER

SEVERN

Purton

N

SITE OF
SEVERN
BRIDGE

M 3

Docks

Sharpness

Wanswell

Berkeley
Road

B 4066

A 38

Miles

River

Berkeley

RJD

ter. Begun in 1793 to enable seagoing sailing ships to by-pass the dangerous lower Severn, it was opened in 1827 with the help of government money. The first ship in was the *Anne*: she was 'admitted into the canal, where she hoisted all her colours, and manned her tops. The towing horses were put to, and' so she arrived at Gloucester. The canal was then the biggest in England, and as big as any in the world. In 1874 a new and much larger entrance and basin were built, taking ships of 5,000 tons.

From the M5 or A38 make for Berkeley on the B4066, and continue to Sharpness. You will pass the *Severn Bridge and Railway Hotel*, its name and sign a reminder that just above Sharpness a single-track railway crossed canal and river on the 22-span Severn Bridge, opened in 1897. In 1959 in fog a tanker hit the bridge and brought down two spans. Later the others were removed and now constitute a road bridge in Chile. Up the towpath is the base of the structure that once carried a steam-powered swing span over the canal. Cross the canal, and park your car beyond.

A path to the right takes you to the old entrance, closed in 1910, now used as boatyard and moorings. Disused ship and barge locks beside former towing horse stables lead to an outer basin and a huge disused tide-lock. Beside is a neo-classical house, an enlarged version of the little houses scattered along the canal for the staff who work the swing bridges (being a ship canal, there are no overhead bridges).

Then walk back to the present docks, as pleasant a mixture of old and new as one could wish to find. Sharpness is its own little community, with villas and cottage rows, cafés, shops, a post office and a bank. Grain and packaged timber are the main cargoes – total tonnage handled was 550,000 in 1975. Courtesy suggests that if you want to have a close look at the docks, you call at the dock office on the north side, near the entrance lock. Craft enter and leave around high tide: therefore choose your time (tide tables in *Whitaker's Almanack*). The tidal range here is thought to be greater than anywhere in the world except the Bay of Fundy.

The canal follows the river wall, with wide views from the towpath, for a mile or so to Purton. There, the *Berkeley Arms* looks across the river to where trains run like models towards Gloucester, while the *Berkeley Hunt*, once a farmhouse, later a boatmen's pub, faces the canal. Refreshed, one can watch the swing bridge being worked, or study the bridgeman's charmingly odd cottage. Two miles further, between canal and river, is the Wildfowl Trust's reserve at Slimbridge, which opens new interests every time I visit it. Over 160 varieties of wildfowl live here, and migrants visit it (enquiries Cambridge (Glos.) 333).

Then, I suggest, to Saul, noting in the village the little coloured figures over several cottage doors. Here the newer Gloucester & Sharpness Canal met and crossed the older Stroudwater Canal (now disused) running from the Severn at Framilode to Stroud, where it joined the Thames & Severn (see No 15). Once the junction was made in 1820, the Saul-Framilode part had little use; the local canal society hopes to reopen it all. Across the ship canal is a disused lock, put in when the junction was made to raise the Stroudwater's level to that of the bigger line.

Should you not have seen the Severn bore, extraordinarily impressive in its spring and autumn power, get F. W. Rowbotham's little book, *The Severn Bore* (David & Charles). It tells you how to work out the bore's time of arrival, and where best to see it.

15

Sapperton Tunnel
Map 163, refs: 965006/943034

A canal pub in the woods, the finest canal tunnel portal in England, a round house, all on a disused canal across the Cotswolds that a local society is working to restore: Sapperton on the Thames & Severn Canal is a must.

The village of Coates near Cirencester is accessible from the A419 or the A433. Thence take the road downhill signposted

Tarlton. After the railway bridge, the canal comes in from the left, one of the five circular round houses once occupied by canal staff lies ahead, and the tunnel approach cutting is to the right. The roof rafters of this round house sloped inwards to the centre, where a leaden bowl collected water that was led out through an opening in the parapet.

Just beyond, the woods begin. First stand on the canal bridge and look at the deep cutting, dark, mysterious, as it approaches the tunnel. Its concrete lining was laid early this century by the county council, who owned it, in an effort to stop leakage. Then follow the lane signposted *Tunnel House Inn* to the pub, solitary in its clearing. It was built while the tunnel was under construction, originally to house workers. The interior was burnt out some years ago, and the old boat-horse stables behind have gone, but the exterior is mostly original, its siting wholly so.

A footpath leads down to the tunnel portal, its arch flanked by niches (never occupied), roundels and Doric columns (for a drawing, see p318 of *CSSEE*). The company probably provided this elaborate design as a tribute to Lord Bathurst, on whose land it stands. As I write, this noble ruin is being restored.

Begun in 1783, after many vicissitudes the tunnel was opened in 1789 when on 20 April the first boat passed through, though a year later the committee sadly noted that 'the Tunnel proves to be very imperfect and leaky in various parts of it'. The engineers were unfortunate in their contractors, more so in the geology with which they had to contend. The limestone through which most of the tunnel passes is full of fissures. These had to be sealed with wooden barriers to prevent canal water escaping; the wood tended to decay and cause leaks. Where, however, the tunnel cut through fuller's earth, any water getting to it caused swelling, so distorting sides and bottom. Most of the canal was abandoned in 1927, and collapses in the tunnel have followed. Peer into the darkness, listen to the eerie dripping and the plop of things that live in the dark water, but don't go in.

Take the road back to Coates and turn left beside the woods on to the A419, then first right for Sapperton, up onto the wolds. You will soon see the spoil heaps beside the road, each crowned by beeches, that mark the sites of vertical shafts (twenty-five were completed) used in cutting the tunnel: one was 244ft deep. Others can be traced back towards *Tunnel House*. Continue down the hill and over the narrow canal bridge to the *Daneway Inn*, formerly the *Bricklayers Arms*, built in 1784. It once faced the summit lock (now under its car park) of the flight leading down to Stroud and on to the Severn. Walk up the towpath to the north-west portal, flanked by its tunnel-keeper's cottage. This end is much plainer, though it once had a row of crenellations punctuated by three small spires. Then take the old horsepath upwards beside the cottage back to the road and so to Daneway again.

Places Nearby
At Daneway note the old wharf cottage, and remains of a small reservoir above the second lock. The towpath is walkable down the locks through the lovely Golden Valley to Chalford: try it in autumn when the leaves are turning.

Or back at the Coates end take the Foss Way to where it crosses the canal (ref: 986990). Park on the slip road, beside which is a canal memorial plaque. The path down past the old wharf house and then beneath the road leads to a huge fenced 63ft-deep well to the right of the towpath, from which a steam engine pumped water for the summit level – the adit runs under the path. A hundred yards further down the Foss Way itself, a field path to the right leads to the source of the Thames: salute it, readers.

16

Rogerstone (Cefn) Locks
Map 171, refs: 288884/278886

Once upon a time, when the Crumlin branch of the Monmouth-shire Canal was busy with iron and coal boats carrying their loads down the Ebbw valley to Newport, they called the country round Allt-yr-yn locks Little Switzerland. That was before the canal died and the M4 came. Yet the flights there and at Rogerstone (Cefn) are in their dereliction still a sight, with something of nobility in their decay.

The Monmouthshire, once out of Newport, forked at Malpas junction (ref: 303894). One line ran north towards the Brecknock & Abergavenny, the other west and then north to Crumlin: this is ours. Half a mile along the towpath from Malpas, the M4 on our right, is the first of the five Allt-yr-yn locks, a little of their charm still clinging to them (for what it was, see the photograph opposite p144 of *CSWB*). A little further on, the bottom lock (No 7) of the Rogerstone (Cefn) flight of fourteen locks lies on the Allt-yr-yn side of the motorway crossing, the 'Fourteen Locks' beyond. Gwent County and Newport Borough Councils have done good work in tidying up the site and allowing water once more to run through the locks. See their Canal Visitor Centre's exhibition (car park and picnic area nearby).

Rogerstone locks are mostly arranged in pairs. But instead of each being a true staircase pair with a common centre gate, a very short pound of half a boat's length or less separates them, so that the top gates of the lower lock and the bottom gates of the upper lock would both have to be open together. Each of these short pounds is connected by a culvert to a large irregularly shaped side-pond or individual reservoir, these being linked also to one another by weirs. This odd arrangement, not quite a staircase, not quite an ordinary flight, seems only to have been used by two engineers, Thomas Dadford junior, as here and elsewhere on the Monmouthshire, and his father who, working for Brindley on the Staffs & Worcs Canal, built three locks at the Bratch like this and a flight very similar to Rogerstone in layout, at the Delph on the Dudley Canal (No 20).

On our way up Rogerstone locks, Nos 10, 11 and 12 constitute a three like the Bratch, linked with two short pounds and side-ponds. But here the centre lock is an oddity, for part way up its height the chamber has been widened to make two shelves, one 5ft down on the towpath side, the other 2ft 6in on the off-side. Some have thought it likely that the extra volume of water it held compensated for a smaller fall than the locks on either side, but measurement shows that this is not so. It must have been provided to enable boats to pass.

There are good views of the flight from Pen-y-Sarn bridge beside Canal Cottage, part way up, or from bridge 6 just off the A467, at the top.

Places Nearby
Using Mr Alan Stevens's excellent towpath guide, I suggest an exploration of the Pontypool branch of the canal upwards from Malpas towards Pontypool and the Brecknock & Abergavenny Canal, by car or on foot. There is much to reward you.

17

Llanfoist Wharf
Map 161, ref: 286130

When I first found Llanfoist, it was a sleeping beauty waiting to be awakened.

The Brecknock (Brecon) & Abergavenny Canal was completed in 1812 as a carrier of coal and iron along the Usk valley, being served by a number of horse tramroads diving down to it from ironworks and collieries in the hills. At Pontypool it joined the Monmouthshire Canal head-on, which ran to Newport. Later, the canals became known jointly as the 'Mon and Brec' – you may still find this title used in guides.

Take the road south from Abergavenny over the Usk to the village of Llanfoist, park by the *Llanfoist Inn*, and pause by the church where the great ironmaster Crawshay Bailey is buried. A narrow road climbs up to the wharf, the top part private property. There a three-storey white house and an old warehouse are held against the backdrop of the tree-clad mountain sides of Blorenge.

Llanfoist was once busy with trade, for three inclined planes brought coal and iron down Hill's horse tramroad from Blaenavon to the wharf for shipment. The tramroad continued over the canal (where the road bridge now is) and by a fourth incline to the valley tramroad that led away to Hereford. Incidentally, the tunnel that leads from the approach road under the canal to the wharf here is an old footpath.

After that first visit of mine the canal, restored through to Brecon, became popular for cruising, and Llanfoist was busy again, house and warehouse renovated, cruisers moored alongside. Then, in 1975, the canal bank gave way nearby and revealed soil instability over several miles of the centre section. I hope that by the time you read this, boats will have returned here. But in any case, visit Llanfoist, not just for what it is, but for what it was, and will be again.

From the wharf I offer two walks: to the agile the path up Blorenge by the old tramroad; to others southwards along the towpath, if possible, for rather over two miles to Ty-coch bridge, where there is easy access to the A4042. This part of the canal south of Gilwern was built by William Crosley junior, an engineer who really understood canals in hilly country. It is a superb example of the canal builder's art, cut out of a hillside that in places steepens towards the vertical, swinging in to meet and cross a mountain stream on a little aqueduct, then out again until the next. Outwards spread superb views, the Usk below, the hills beyond.

Places Nearby

I suggest a drive to Brecon. Make first for Gilwern, where the A465 bridge over the canal (ref: 246145) has the *Bridgend Inn* at one end, the *Navigation* at the other, and the *Lion* just up the road. Then walk along the towpath over the very high (some 75ft) embankment across the Clydach valley. At the far end a lane to the left leads to the old Glangroyne tramroad track that runs under the embankment in a tunnel. A footpath will take you back to the *Lion*.

The A4077 runs to Llangattock and the B4558 then parallels the canal almost to Brecon. By Cwm Crawnon it crosses the canal (ref: 146199), where one may walk up the four Llangynidr locks that lie above the bridge (there is another below). These, not long restored, are of the special South Wales size of some 65ft × 9$\frac{1}{2}$ft. Because the top locks are very close together, a side-pond storing additional water is connected to the canal by a culvert.

Still following the B4558, look at the modest Ashford tunnel (ref: 123216) alongside the road and wonder why, with so little above it, a tunnel was ever made. And so to Talybont (ref: 113228), a real canal village. From the wharf with its row of disused limekilns you can follow the old Brynoer tramroad back into the hills.

Stop just before the A40 outside Brecon (map 160, ref: 077273). To your left is the top lock, a charming cottage beside it; to the right the four-arched Brynich masonry aqueduct that takes the canal over the Usk, solid and wide, unpretentious, with massive cutwaters to the piers.

18

Stourport-on-Severn
Map 138, ref: 810710

The canal made Stourport. The few houses of Lower Mitton lay where the Stour, running down through Kidderminster, joined the Severn. This was England's busiest river, navigable upwards past Bridgnorth and Coalbrookdale to Shrewsbury and beyond, downwards to Worcester, Gloucester and the Bristol Channel, when in 1766 James Brindley and Thomas Dadford began to build the Staffordshire & Worcestershire Canal. A narrow-boat line, at its northern end it joined the Trent & Mersey at Great Haywood (No 30); in the centre it had links with Birmingham; here in the south it joined the Severn, so giving the Midlands a waterway down to Gloucester and Bristol. The digging of the first Stourport basin was begun in 1768. It was used by 1771 and the whole canal opened in 1772. Thus Stourport was created out of Lower Mitton.

Now, canalside Stourport is a place within a place. As one approaches it along York Street from Bridge Street and the town, one first crosses the canal beside a deep lock and Victorian gothic tollhouse built in 1853. Painted canalware and souvenirs can be bought here. Below, Middle Basin, the biggest and oldest of the four remaining basins (there were once six) opens out, on one side a long red-brick warehouse surmounted by a clocktower, on the other a maintenance yard and behind it the *Tontine Hotel*, which faces the Severn on its far side. Beyond the *Tontine*, a broad lock leads to a lower basin which through a second lock joins the Severn, the *Angel* beside it. To the west two other interconnected basins, Clock Basin behind the clock warehouse and another below it, are joined to each other and the river by staircase pairs of narrow locks.

The clock was put on what was then a new warehouse by the inhabitants of Stourport in 1812, the canal company contributing £25. The *Tontine* was built mainly to serve businessmen drawn by canal activity and provide a meeting place for committeemen and shareholders. It is shown in a print of 1776. Its name implies that it was paid for with money raised in that gruesome kind of lottery in which subscribers took tickets for their healthiest young children: he who lived longest took the property. The central part is still a many-roomed pub; the rest, private houses. Looked at from the front, the windowscape is delightfully odd.

The basins, once busy with commercial craft, became deserted; now they are busy once more, but with pleasure boats. There are always plenty here, and boatyards to serve them.

Places Nearby
In Stourport's main street look for the sign of the *Severn Trow*. It shows *Norah*, built at Bridgwater, Somerset, in 1866.

From the tail of the lower barge lock you can walk downstream past the remains of river wharves on the old horse towing path. About 1¼ miles of walking will bring you to the uppermost lock of the Severn itself, Lincomb.

Less than three miles up the Severn is Bewdley, once a flourishing river port, its warehouses, merchants' houses and pubs along the riverside quays full of eighteenth-century charm, its river bridge built by Telford in 1798. In the early eighteenth century Bewdley and Wribbenhall across the river were important inland ports, for slight tides and deeper water ran this far. So at Bewdley cargoes from downstream were transhipped to smaller craft to go on up the Severn to Bridgnorth, Ironbridge or Shrewsbury, and to road waggons for the Midlands. Other cargoes returned downwards. Then the basins of Stourport replaced Bewdley, whose trade slowly declined, though the last commercial boat left its wharves only in 1941.

19

Tardebigge Locks
Map 139, ref: 995693

Tardebigge offers much besides locks. Nevertheless, locks are the sight – the biggest flight in the country. A flight usually means a succession of locks each within 200yds of the next. In this sense there are twenty-nine but, given not much greater intervals, one could add Tardebigge top lock and the six more of the Stoke flight, making a fall of 259ft.

From the top lock at Tardebigge the Worcester & Birmingham Canal runs level through four tunnels to Gas Street, Birmingham (No 22). This top lock is unusually deep, for a reason. When the canal was building in the early 1790s, it looked as if the company would have to pump water for their Tardebigge–Birmingham summit level all the way from the Severn. So when John Woodhouse offered to build an experimental vertical lift at Tardebigge at his own expense, if the company paid for excavation and masonry, they were delighted, for a lift would use almost no water. It was ready in June 1808 (a picture faces p144 of *CWM*). A wooden tank took a narrow boat and was counterbalanced by a platform loaded with bricks, the two being connected by chains passing over eight cast-iron wheels. Wooden gates sealed each end of tank and canal. The tank was wound up and down by two men. It worked well, but Rennie advised that such lifts would not be robust enough for years of rough service, and management agreed. And so, helped by a supply of water which had now been arranged for, locks were built instead and only Tardebigge top lock, built beside the lift site, remains to remind us of an early experiment, A pity, for I would love to sit on Tardebigge slope and watch boatmen winding a series of Woodhouse lifts up and down.

Above the top lock, a maintenance yard lies to the left at

Tardebigge wharf. Beyond is Tardebigge tunnel, 580yds long, the first of the four. If you go through by boat, you will see the magnificent rock strata; or you can walk over it on the horse-path. Because this canal was originally planned to carry barges, its tunnels and bridge-holes on the summit level are all broad, though the locks are narrow. Beyond its far end is a boatyard at Tardebigge Old Wharf.

A walk down the locks offers endless changes of view as the canal drops towards Stoke Prior. The top lock is No 58, for there are fifty-eight altogether in the sixteen miles to the Severn at Worcester. Below it, oddly, the former pumping engine-house is now a restaurant and night club. Over a bank beside locks 54 to 50 is the smallish Tardebigge reservoir, popular with fishermen. Beside it stands a ruined enginehouse, now without its steam engine. I love such a walk as this: each lock is a little different – some with a cottage, or a bridge, or some quirk to distinguish it. Every now and then one meets a cruiser being worked up, and has a happy time comparing techniques – admiring some, tut-tutting at others. At the bottom of Tardebigge 30 is the *Queen's Head* (map 150, ref: 962679) where one can sit to recover before finishing the job with Stoke 6 to Stoke Wharf (map 150, ref: 670952). By car, take the A448 from Tardebigge towards Droitwich and then the B4091. Stoke Wharf is a pleasant little canal hamlet, complete with warehouse, crane, cottages and pub. A mile north, off the B4091, is the Avoncroft Museum of Buildings, where historic houses and industrial structures are re-erected and opened to the public (enquiries Bromsgrove 31363).

Stoke Works is further on. When salt was found here in 1825, John Corbett planned the works to use canal transport for coal coming in and salt going out. They are closed now, replaced by chemicals. But, beyond the works, by bridge 42 (map 150, ref: 944663) is the nicely named *Boat and Railway*, canal in front and railway behind. After a strenuous day one can sit outside it and see the boats going by – in what better way can one watch the shadows lengthen?

Delph Locks to Netherton Tunnel
Map 139

This is the tunnel route: past one of the earliest and certainly the most extraordinary, Dudley tunnel; one that has been opened out, Brewin's; and what was until 1974 the newest and is still the largest, Netherton. But not only tunnels. The scene is, of course, industrial, but much is surprisingly open with fine views, and some is reclaimed and newly landscaped land. It is a five-mile walk, but points of interest can be visited by car with the help of a street atlas.

The foot of the eight Delph locks (ref: 917865) on the Dudley No 1 Canal line is reached from Brierley Hill. This flight delights me every time I see it, for the overflow water from the top and intermediate pounds, instead of running in open or covered channels round the locks, cascades down rusticated open falls. Once, nine locks with irregular side-ponds curved up here, arranged much like Rogerstone (No 16). In 1858 they were replaced by eight, the top and bottom locks of the old flight being retained and six new ones built. Nevertheless, the area round is still called Nine Locks. Traces of old locks can be seen to the right as one looks up.

A mile above the locks the canal passes through Round Oak steelworks, an astonishing sight. Just beyond, to the right, the towpath bridges nothing. This is Woodside Junction and a short canal, the Two Lock Line, ran under it to meet the Dudley No 2 Canal three furlongs away across the valley at Blackbrook. Heavy mining subsidence closed it in 1909 and now, as we look across, it seems impossible that once a canal spanned the considerable valley.

We soon come to Blower's Green lock (deep because it replaced two old ones) and beyond it a junction. To the left rise the three Park Head locks, restored and reopened in 1973. Beyond, past the disused private Pensnett Canal to the left, lies that very odd tunnel, 1¾ miles long, the Dudley (ref: 933893). With no towpath, the small-bore bricked sections of tunnel are broken by limestone caves, old tunnel branches, and the silent expanse of Castle Mill basin, former limestone quarry, open to the sky (tunnel plan, *CWM*, p78). The line runs right under Dudley town and castle, to come out beside the site where the imaginative Black Country Museum is being created to reproduce the region's history in microcosm. There are no ventilation shafts, so internal combustion engines are not allowed: party boats are taken through, legged by volunteers or electric powered, by the Dudley Canal Trust (enquiries 021-440-4357).

Back at Blower's Green let us take the Dudley No 2 Canal line, opened in 1798 from here to the Worcester & Birmingham Canal at Selly Oak. Fine views open to the right; on the left is Netherton church, where graves are said to be cut in solid coal. High Bridge, a mile further on, spans a considerable cutting. Regular walling here marks where 75yd long Brewin's tunnel, built in 1858 as part of a shortening scheme, was later opened out. Brewin was the canal's superintendent at the time. Some way on, the Bumblehole branch opens to the left, leading now to a boatyard. It was once part of a loop of the Dudley's line until the construction of Netherton tunnel. When the embankment was built it took a more direct route across the valley to Windmill End Junction. To the right the Dudley No 2 line reaches out to Gosty Hill tunnel. The rest has ceased to be navigable but can still be traced as far as the *Black Horse* inn on Manor Way. To the left is the Boshboil arm, the other end of the Bumblehole loop, ahead is Netherton's curving blue-brick abutments and wide mouth (ref: 954884).

Until the new tunnels on the Birmingham Main Line (No 21) were opened in 1974 and 1975, Netherton was Britain's youngest canal tunnel, opened in 1858; $1\frac{3}{4}$ miles long, wide enough for boats to pass, with double towpaths and, when built, gas lighting. As part of the same 1858 improvement the Bumblehole loop was by-passed and Brewin's tunnel opened out, the Two Lock line cut and Delph locks rebuilt. The tunnel's other end leads straight to Dudley Port Junction and the Birmingham Main Line.

21

Birmingham: Oldbury Locks to Brasshouse Lane
Map 139

I have chosen this walk of under three miles for the interest of its canalscape (it includes two canal flyovers, a new tunnel, a canal with a motorway roof, and the country's finest cast-iron canal bridge and oldest working narrow locks) and for its demonstration of how our forefathers met pressure for more efficient transport.

Take the Smethwick road out of Birmingham and when approaching Oldbury turn left into Pope's Lane – Engine Street, Oldbury, is its continuation – or take buses 125 or 126 from Birmingham's central bus station to the *Navigation*. At Engine Street we are just below the top lock of the Oldbury flight of six that fall from the Titford Canal down to the Wolverhampton (473ft) level of the Birmingham Canal Navigations. Side-ponds flank the locks, and a simple single-storey lockhouse stands at the bottom.

Down at the canal junction, turn right along a re-aligned section that weaves in and out of a pillared tangle under the M5. This is Brindley's original Birmingham Canal that was opened through Wolverhampton to the Staffs & Worcs Canal in 1772. A brick roving bridge – it transfers the towpath – stands oddly under the motorway. Soon our canal crosses the later BCN Main Line on the Steward aqueduct; beside it huge motorway supports spring from the lower canal bed. Brick with stone quoins on arches and abutments, and a string course above, we shall see this aqueduct better from below. It was built to carry Brindley's line when in the 1820s Telford cut a wide, straight and level modern canal beneath it.

Beyond Steward aqueduct to the left, the three Spon Lane locks lead down to what is now the Main Line, but was originally part of the Wednesbury branch, whence Birmingham got its first canal-borne coal. They are reckoned the oldest narrow locks still working, for they are Brindley's and date from 1769. Once there were six, for they continued up Smethwick hill to the 491ft level. First Brindley proposed to tunnel the hill; then, finding the ground bad, he substituted six locks up from the Wednesbury branch, and six down again at the far end. As traffic increased, so these lock flights became congested, and in 1789 Smeaton laid out a new canal through a 46ft deep cutting at the 473ft level south of the old line to bring our Wolverhampton line into the new summit and eliminate three locks at each end. His line continues on to the right.

Let us turn left and walk down Spon Lane locks past the iron split bridge at the tail of the top lock, designed to pass a towline between its two halves. At the foot of the locks, as we turn sharp left onto the Main Line, stand two graceful Horseley Ironworks roving bridges. This Main Line at 453ft was built to cut right through Smethwick hill. In its day Telford's great cutting, 71ft at its deepest, gave Birmingham the 1830s equivalent of an arterial road – a broad lockless canal with double towpaths. As we stroll along, it is difficult to picture the waterway crowded with horse-drawn boats, and without most of the obstructions to a clear view that it has since acquired. Nevertheless, these have their own interest.

First we walk beneath the M5, then under the Steward aqueduct and, second bridge from Steward, Spon Lane road bridge, probably Telford's, with its abutments flared towards the bottom and iron railings. Round a curve is a railway bridge, and then Telford's magnificent cast-iron 150ft-span Galton bridge. Just beyond, piercing through the embankment carrying a new road in a huge concrete pipe, is a new canal tunnel, 123yds long, complete with towpath and railings, opened in 1974. (A second tunnel, opened in 1975, lies above it on the 473ft line.) The next bridge carries Brasshouse Lane: just before it, beside the towpath, is a pumphouse where once water that had been used at Spon Lane and Smethwick locks was returned to the Wolverhampton level.

Further on we reach Telford's single-arched iron fly-over aqueduct that takes the Engine Branch over the Main Line from the Wolverhampton level. An iron trough supported from beneath by a cast-iron arch bridge carries the water channel, but the towpath and equivalent space on the far side are borne on delicate iron arched supports, an object lesson in how the utilitarian could be given delights to offer passers-by – in this case mainly boatmen.

A canal island follows where once a toll-collector's office stood, and then more Horseley bridges as we reach Smethwick Junction and turn back up the three Smethwick locks. These date from 1789, but on their right are traces of Brindley's originals. Pleasant old brick paths lead up beside them, ridged at intervals to give horses a grip, and to the right is the *Old Navigation* pub.

Beyond the top lock we can walk over the Engine Arm aqueduct on its brick-barred towpath, before continuing to Brasshouse Lane bridge past, of all BCN oddities, a piggery. Standing on the far side of the bridge and looking west, the Main Line lies below us, the Wolverhampton level alongside, and to our right and above, children are walking along a path that marks the level of the original summit. Here we have the three canals, of 1769, 1789 and 1829, Brindley's, Smeaton's and Telford's, monuments of transport history.

Cross the bridge and the railway footbridge for bus B86 which will return you to Pope's Lane.

22

Birmingham: Gas Street, Farmer's Bridge and The Long Boat
Map 139

In spite of its name, Gas Street is a romantic place. I came to it last in a March drizzle, to see jumbled buildings, a double line of painted narrow boats moored endways on to Worcester Bar, smoke rising from their chimneys, boat families looking out, a dog pleased to see a visitor. Gas Street may be redeveloped and has already been partly opened out, but just now it is not unlike what it was fifty years ago, and about the only place where one can see so many narrow boats together.

Gas Street turns off Broad Street, a few minutes' walk from New Street in central Birmingham. Down it, a small opening in

Gas Street Basin, Birmingham

a wall on the left leads to the towpath beside canal cottages and former stables. Facing, a stop-lock is permanently open; on its far side is the masonry barrier of Worcester Bar. To the right the Worcester & Birmingham Canal runs for thirty miles past King's Norton (No 23) and Tardebigge (No 19) to the Severn; to the left the Birmingham Canal Navigations begin. The Bar was once really a bar. When the W & B was first promoted around 1790, the older Birmingham company realised that, with its heavy lockage down to the Severn, the W & B would be water-thirsty. The busy Birmingham needed all its own, for water is the circulating life-blood of a canal system, and cannot be allowed to bleed away. So the Bar was built, transhipment being by crane over the wall. Circumstances slowly changed and in 1815 it was breached by a stop-lock, though only in exchange for substantial compensation tolls on all goods passing.

Let us now walk under what is called Broad Street tunnel, but is really an echoing hugely extended brick bridge. On the far side is a canal junction, sharp left Oozells Street loop, part of Brindley's 1769 Birmingham Canal, half left the Main Line towards Smethwick (No 21), and right the Birmingham & Fazeley Canal. This is ours, over a Horseley Ironworks roving bridge. A few yards ahead are two charming white towpath cottages, a little tollhouse, and the first lock of the Farmer's Bridge flight. Across the water, past the moored cruisers, is *The Long Boat* pub. There is no access from the towpath, but we shall get there in the end.

Farmer's Bridge locks are an experience. Here is this flight – the thirteen locks date from the late 1780s – with its narrow-boat chambers, white-tipped lock beams, cramped side-ponds and cobbled walkways, dropping down between and under modern Birmingham, two centuries coexisting. Because the locks are crowded, some having very short intermediate pounds, side-ponds are not just reservoirs but passing places also. Some have now been partially built over, so that water stretches away into blackness like a Venice of the factories. Each has its weir, usually circular, to carry its surplus water underground and by mysterious routes beneath roads, buildings or, in one case, a house, to supply the pound below: the sound of rushing water accompanies your descent. Daylight recedes. One lock is partly in a short tunnel, another under the concrete pillars of a new building where one notes iron bars fixed to the underside of the floor above for use when lock gates have to be lifted out.

Endless bridges cross the line. The Post Office tower rises up, the Birmingham Museum of Science and Industry peers down, a telephone exchange encloses a thousand voices, the old Snow Hill station site, now built over, runs above. The flight ends on a short level line to Aston Junction. From here six Ashted locks and a little tunnel take the Digbeth branch to Bordesley and the Grand Union for London, or eleven Aston locks run down to Salford (canal) junction beneath Spaghetti (motorway) junction. From Salford the Birmingham & Fazeley continues towards the Coventry or the Trent & Mersey. We return up the flight, however, to see the whole extraordinary sight in reverse.

Just past the lock cottages at the top of the flight, try the wooden door into the street. If it is locked, then where the roving bridge leads back to Gas Street, see if there is still access to the neighbouring car park. If so, you can get into it, turn right onto the road and then first left to Kingston Row and *The Long Boat*. If not, we must return by the towpath to Gas Street, then cross Broad Street and walk by St Peter's Place and St Martin's Place to Cambridge Street. Turn left, and on your right you will find Kingston Row, its old ochre-coloured canal cottages restored, one now a canal shop and information centre. To the right is *The Long Boat* on Cambrian Wharf. Behind, tower blocks of flats are sited sensibly in relation to the canal. The pub's surroundings have been pleasantly handled, and include two old cranes. Outside, a narrow boat in a small dock serves as an extra bar; inside, the very canalish layout, with seating divided by butty rudders and helms, has the merit of using many genuine bits and pieces, including a Bolinder engine, maps and photographs. Outside, the balcony is a good place to sit and look at boats. What better occupation when not using them?

The area's development exemplifies a change in the attitude of city councils, who once despised the decayed industrial waterways that criss-crossed their territories, and now think them valuable aids to amenity development.

Passenger trips are run in the summer from Gas Street (enquiries 021-643-8397).

23

King's Norton Stop-lock
Map 139, ref: 055794

King's Norton lock is on the northern Stratford-upon-Avon Canal, near its junction with the Worcester & Birmingham Canal, $5\frac{3}{4}$ miles south of Gas Street, Birmingham (No 22).

Each canal company used to hoard water, for without enough of it fully loaded boats could not move. Where one canal joined another, therefore, a stop-lock was built to separate each company's water and enable its use to be controlled. Vertically rising or guillotine lock gates are uncommon on rivers (they can be seen, for example on the Nene), even more so on canals: King's Norton is the only guillotine-gated stop-lock. The wooden gates, held in iron frames, were formerly raised by chains passing over wheels to counterweights. Once nationalisation enabled water to move freely within the canal system, the gates were kept raised, and now lack some parts.

The 1793 Act for the Stratford Canal provided for a lock with four pairs of gates, two facing each way, to enable boats to be worked whether the water in the Stratford was higher or lower than in the Worcester & Birmingham. The Stratford was intended as a barge, not a narrow-boat canal. It is likely, therefore, that the stop-lock was originally broad, and was subsequently narrowed, for on the towpath side the coping is of cut sandstone and probably original, but on the other side is of brick. One guesses that guillotine gates were provided when the lock was narrowed, probably in 1815–20, and probably by William Whitmore, who built the iron aqueducts lower down (No 24). As he was a weighbridge builder, it seems in his line.

Places Nearby
A short distance down the Stratford's towpath at ref: 066794 is

Brandwood tunnel (352yds) through which men hauled craft using a fixed hand-rail. Over the entrance is Shakespeare's head between laurel sprays in a medallion. Beyond bridge 7 (ref: 102781) is the sizeable single-arched brick aqueduct that carries the canal over the river Cole and Aqueduct Road. Just beyond is a windlass-worked steel lift bridge, by the former *Boatman's Rest* pub (ref: 103779). By bridge 16 (ref: 115751) the navigable feeder enters from Earlswood lakes (canal reservoirs) totalling 85 acres of water. Here there is walking on public footpaths, fishing and sailing, plenty of birds to see, and a nature trail round 40 acres of coppice.

Back at the junction, with its good brick canal house, note the metal plaque with SND 5¾ miles (from Birmingham). The letters stand for Sharpness New Docks, the company controlling the Gloucester & Sharpness ship canal, who bought the Worcester & Birmingham in 1874.

From there you can take the Worcester & Birmingham's towpath going south. Past bridge 70 is a turning bay for the steam tugs that formerly worked the tunnel we are approaching; from the bridge one can see their coaling buildings, ahead and on the side opposite the towpath. Then follows ornate bridge 71, and the entrance to West (Wast) Hill tunnel, 2,726yds (ref: 047779). Opened in 1797, 'the execution of which', a newspaper said, 'had been a matter of ridicule as an almost impossible scheme', tunnel tugs hauled boats through it till 1955. Beyond the tunnel, is Lower Bittell reservoir (ref: 020740) beside and below the canal, here on an embankment. On the reservoir's north side the feeder (once navigable) comes in from Upper Bittell reservoir, beside the red-brick cottage. It's a pleasant place for a picnic.

24

Three Iron-trough Aqueducts: Bearley, Wootton Wawen, Yarningale
Map 151

Bearley (or Edstone) iron-trough narrow-boat aqueduct (ref:

162608) is a very remarkable structure. At 521ft second longest of the breed after Pontcysyllte (No 28), its towpath is not carried above the waterway as it is there, but alongside it, as with the older Longdon-on-Tern aqueduct on the disused Shrewsbury Canal.

Bearley was built in 1815, the creation of the engineer of the southern section of the Stratford-upon-Avon Canal, William Whitmore, and the company's superintendent, William James. Whitmore was a Birmingham engineer and manufacturer of scales, weighbeams and other ironwork. James was a land agent by profession, a waterway and railway enthusiast by choice; his was the drive that got the southern section of the Stratford open by 1816. He was also for a time the owner of the Upper Avon.

In 1814 Whitmore asked the canal committee whether he should build short approach embankments and a long aqueduct or *vice versa*. They chose a long aqueduct as likely to be cheaper, and so Bearley's fourteen-arched trough strides across a wide valley that carries a road, stream and railway. It is plain, solid and rather striking, one side showing rectangular iron plates bolted together, the other the iron railings of the towpath. Trough and towpath are carried upon brick piers with stone cappings. Underneath, iron webs support the trough and link the piers.

An attractive walk north of just over a mile takes you from Bearley in one small river valley to Wootton Wawen in another, by the isolated 'odd lock' and through two cuttings. At Wootton Wawen the iron trough (ref: 159629) carries the canal over the A34 on two brick piers, the type of pier and position of the tow-path being similar to Bearley. A plaque on the side reads 'This aqueduct was erected by the Stratford Canal Compy in October, 1813, Bernard Dewes Esqr Chairman W. James Esqr Depy Chairman W. Whitmore Engineer'. Just above is the *Navigation* inn ('navigation' meaning a canal navigation, the old term for a canal) and beside it a sizeable basin, now a hire-cruiser base.

And so to Yarningale by way of Preston Bagot on the B4095 at ref: 173654. If we follow the towpath thence up the canal to the north east, past lock 38, we reach lock 37 and one of the barrel-roofed lock cottages peculiar to this southern section of the Stratford Canal. The roof construction is a semicircle of brick supported by a tied framework of iron that lies on top of the house walls. This odd way to build a house is likely to have been the brain-child of William Whitmore, whom one guesses to have loved anything with iron in it. One of the dottier canal legends is that such cottages were built by men more used to building tunnels than houses.

Three more locks bring us to another barrel-roofed lockhouse and Yarningale at ref: 184664. The small single-arched aqueduct is not the original, which was washed away in a great storm on the night of 28 July 1834. This new iron trough, similar in design to the others we have seen and therefore probably made from the original drawings, was manufactured so quickly by the Horseley Ironworks that the canal reopened on 23 August. What was built so rapidly has stood well for a century and a half.

25

The Hay Inclined Plane
Map 127, ref: 695027

Thanks to the Ironbridge Gorge Museum Trust, a unique structure can now be seen beside the river Severn at Coalport, a reconstructed canal inclined plane that once raised boats over 200ft from near river level.

An inclined plane is an ingenious device that enables boats to be carried in wheeled trucks running on rails up a slope from one level to another. In former days twenty-seven such planes were built on canals in Great Britain. They were especially useful to canals built through hilly country, for they saved the time of working through a long flight of locks as well as the water that would be used.

The Hay inclined plane on the old small-gauge or tub-boat Shropshire Canal at Coalport has a vertical rise of 207ft in a horizontal distance of some 1,000ft and is equivalent to about twenty-seven average locks. It took boats carrying five tons.

How it worked –
Top of incline

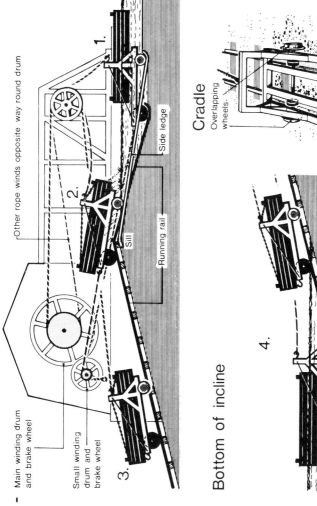

Other rope winds opposite way round drum

Main winding drum and brake wheel

Small winding drum and brake wheel

Side ledge

Running rail

Sill

1.

2.

3.

Cradle

Overlapping wheels.

Bottom of incline

4.

There is a good view of it from the Coalport-Jackfield river footbridge. Opened in 1792, the incline was last used in 1894 after just over a century of service; the Museum Trust have now restored it roughly to its state then.

The accompanying sketches show how the inclined plane worked. It had two parallel rail tracks, each with a boat-carrying cradle, one being at the top when the other was at the bottom. The two cradles were linked by a rope (later a chain) running round a winding drum connected to a steam engine. A tricky little problem occurred at the top of the plane, where the up-coming cradle had to pass over the sill at the top and down the short reverse slope into the upper pound of the canal. To deal with this, and still keep the boat fairly level so that part of the cargo should not fall out, the cradle was given front wheels (27in dia) bigger than the rear ones (16in) for running on the main slope. But on the same axle as the small 16in wheels were two others of 24in dia. As the cradle came over the sill, these picked up a special set of iron-surfaced ledges fastened to the walls of the upper dock, and so prevented the boat tipping up. At the top and bottom of the incline the cradle ran down into a dock where, after its lashings had been removed, the boat it carried could be floated off.

At the bottom of the plane, the canal did not join the Severn: instead, it turned sharply east and ran parallel to and above the river for ¾ mile. Between the two were warehouses and wharves for exchanging cargoes with river craft.

Below the restored Hay incline, the lower dock and basin have been filled with water. To the east the old bed can be followed towards Coalport bridge. Nearby is the entrance to the Tar tunnel (see the Trust's separate leaflet). The slope of the incline has now been relaid with bullhead rails of the type used in the final twenty years of its service. Part way up, the slope crosses over the old railway to Coalport. At the top, the upper basin has been watered, and the dock's cradle rails and iron surfaced ledges of the reverse slope can be seen.

Beyond the head of the plane are the 42 acres of the Blists Hill Open Air Museum, with entrance off the Coalport-Madeley road at ref: 693034. A section of the old tub-boat canal through it has been restored, and two stop-locks, a tub-boat and an ice-breaker can be seen. Further up the road, to the left, the *All Nations* is one of the few pubs in the country that brew their own beer.

Places Nearby
The 'must' is the Iron Bridge (ref: 672034) and the early remains of Coalbrookdale Ironworks, where iron was first smelted with coal (instead of charcoal), the crucial discovery that began the industrial revolution. (Information from the Ironbridge Gorge Museum Trust, Church Hill, Ironbridge, Telford, Salop, TF8 7RE.)

26

Ellesmere and its Lakes
Map 126, ref: 398344

Ellesmere has its own canal-served lake district: not perhaps comparable to that in Cumbria, but one which took my breath away with its spring beauty when I first cruised the Llangollen Canal and found it.

This little town gave its name to the ambitious Ellesmere Canal that was to run from the Mersey via Wrexham and Ruabon to Shrewsbury. The line that got built was rather different, but it included the Wirral Canal from Chester to the Mersey. When a new town began to grow round this canal's Merseyside locks, it took its name of Ellesmere Port from the canal company, and so indirectly from here.

A short branch off the Llangollen line runs to the town basin. Old warehouses and cranes face big dairy buildings, where they are not above filling a boater's jug with milk in the intervals of handling their thousands of gallons. One warehouse still carries a faded legend from the days before 1922 when the Shropshire Union Railways & Canal Co carried goods from here by water. A maintenance yard stands at the junction, beside it the curved brick frontage of Beech House, once the canal company's headquarters, now private houses.

A short way down the towpath to the east, where the A528 crosses the canal (ref: 412340) is the 87yd-long Ellesmere tunnel, with an iron-railed path through. Beyond on the left lies Blake Mere, one of nine charming lakes in the area. Blake Mere (with tiny Kettle Mere just beyond it) is hill-bounded, quiet and wooded, ideal for a picnic, to watch the birds on the lake or the canal's passing craft. Beyond, this time on the right of the canal and below its level, is the larger but equally beautiful Cole Mere. Two old limekilns can be found here in the woods by the canal. From the canal bridge just before the mere (ref: 428335), a footpath runs down the mere's southern side to Colemere village. Fishermen can obtain day tickets for either mere (or others) in Ellesmere. On the edge of Ellesmere itself is the biggest of the lakes, The Mere, covering 116 acres, after which the town is named. There is boating and fishing here, while on the town side one can sit and watch the water from pretty Cremorne Gardens.

Places Nearby
I suggest the double canal junction at Frankton (ref: 371318), reached from Ellesmere by the A495 towards Whittington, and the by-road through Welsh Frankton. From the road bridge over the canal, a short walk eastwards brings one to the junction, where four ruined locks, the first two a staircase pair crossed by a little iron bridge, lead steeply downwards. If we follow the path past them and on, we shall soon come to a canal T-junction, a derelict canal running each way. As we saw, the original Ellesmere Canal line of the 1790s was intended to run from the Mersey via Chester, Wrexham and Ruabon to Shrewsbury. From Pontcysyllte near Ruabon (No 28) higher up the Llangollen Canal, therefore, the canal ran this way to Frankton junction, turned down the ruined locks, and then left at the T-junction on its way to Shrewsbury, though it got no nearer than Westonwharf (ref: 420257) where a warehouse, limekilns and other structures can still be found by the old basin. To the right at the T-junction was the Ellesmere Canal branch to Carreghofa, where it met the surpassingly beautiful Montgomeryshire Canal (No 27) that ran onwards through Welshpool to Newtown. The restoration of parts of the Montgomeryshire Canal has now

begun, and we may hope that before too long the canal from Frankton will once again be open to boats seeking the upper Severn valley.

27

Montgomeryshire Canal:
Carreghofa via Welshpool to Berriew
Maps 126, 136

The disused Montgomeryshire Canal, to my mind one of Britain's loveliest, offers a scenic day out in Shropshire and Powys. Abandoned in 1944, seven miles of it near Welshpool are now being restored and there is good hope that one day it will again be open throughout.

The previous 'sight', No 26, took us to Frankton's ruined narrow locks branching off the Llangollen Canal at ref: 371318. From the T-junction below them the former Ellesmere Canal's branch to Carreghofa, 11 miles long, began. Thence the Montgomeryshire Canal continued to Pool Quay, Welshpool, and up the steep-sided Severn valley to Newtown. Later, both Ellesmere and Montgomeryshire became part of the Shropshire Union Canal system, a name still used on OS maps. Let us therefore begin where the true Montgomeryshire began, 35yds north of the upper of the two Carreghofa locks, ref: 255203, just off the B4398. A little single-storey slated tollhouse stands here, a verandah in front supported on two slender pillars. Above the locks, a water feeder from the Tanat river comes in, necessary to the restoration work further on, and a two-storey lockhouse stands by the road. Half a mile on, the canal crosses the Vyrnwy.

The Montgomeryshire's engineers and contractors were experienced men, and yet the long, low masonry structure of the Vyrnwy aqueduct with its five river and three flood (land) arches has caused endless trouble. It had hardly been built before part of an arch collapsed in 1796. Later, subsidence affected it and in 1823 every arch was reported fractured; it was then given a variety of tie-rods and iron braces. It leaked then, it has leaked since, and from time to time it leaks now. Incidentally, at the Canal Exhibition Centre at Llangollen Wharf there are models of the building of the aqueduct and of Carreghofa locks.

You can reach Burgedin locks (ref: 252147) from the Vyrnwy aqueduct by B4393, A483 and B4392. Just above the locks, the two-mile long Guilsfield branch goes off to end at Tyddyn (ref: 229125), where ruined wharf buildings still await their boats – uselessly, for the branch is planned to become a nature reserve, and so not to be restored. After the two locks the canal crosses a valley on the Wern embankment to Bank lock, and begins a steady climb to keep pace with the rising level of the valley. The A483 parallels it all the way.

Pool Quay (ref: 256116) sees canal and Severn close together. Given enough water in the river, this was the highest point to which barges could be brought on the Severn. The canal is now being restored from Ardd-lin (Arddleen) a mile the far side of Burgedin locks through here to Gallowstree bridge below Welshpool. Above the bridge, the trip-boat *Powis Princess* runs from the town wharf.

In the 1820s and early 1830s the canal had the lively G.W. Buck as engineer. He reckoned that wooden lock-gates had had their day and, as replacements were required, put in curved iron ones with plain iron to iron mitre facings where the two gates meet. The pair that he put into Welshpool lock in 1832, with his name on the sill, is now at the Waterways Museum at Stoke Bruerne (No 56), fitted to the lock that has the weighing machine. Sadly, no others remain. He probably also designed the sturdy pattern of ground paddle gear to be found, eg at Belan, which works paddles laid horizontally in the canal bed.

Beyond Welshpool, a quick look at the two Belan locks with their pleasant lockhouse (ref: 215052), and on to the small iron-trough aqueduct over the river Luggy at Brithdir (map 136, ref: 198023). The iron trough with its nice balustrade was installed in 1820, replacing an earlier, probably masonry, structure. Let us end our visit with the massive Berriew aqueduct over the Rhiw at ref: 189006. The original had two river and two land arches. It was replaced in 1889 by the present one in brickwork, with two main river arches and a smaller road arch on either side. And so ends a day that I hope has pleased you. It has me. If, however, you have the time to explore more of the canal, hanging to its hillside as it winds towards Newtown, you will be well rewarded.

28

Pontcysyllte Aqueduct
Map 117, ref: 271421

Can anyone forget his first passage on the Llangollen Canal over Pontcysyllte aqueduct? In a boat you come on it at short view along a high bushy embankment. Suddenly, almost sickeningly, the land falls into the deep, wild valley of the Dee, and your boat is floating in the air. It is launched upon the iron trough of the 1,007ft long aqueduct. On the right the towpath, low-railed on its outer side, is cantilevered over the trough. On the left is a sheer drop of 126ft at maximum. The height is hard to grasp. Morning sun throws the shadow of slim tapering piers and tiny trough right across the valley floor. A little moving hump in the trough line shadow is your boat.

From the old road bridge far below you can best appreciate this aerial masterpiece, highest canal aqueduct in the world. (If you pronounce it Pont-ker-silter you won't be far wrong.) Its eighteen slender tapering stone piers cross the valley, locally quarried. Work began in 1795. A cast-iron tablet on a pier on the Vron side tells you: 'The navigation over this Aqueduct was opened 26th November, 1805'. Throughout almost the whole period Britain had been at war against Napoleon, but daring and invention had not slackened.

The principal engineer of the canal was William Jessop; his resident engineer, Thomas Telford, was twelve years younger. No-one will succeed in accurately apportioning the credit for Pontcysyllte between them. We know, however, that Jessop took sole responsibility to the canal company for the proposal to build an iron trough aqueduct at full height across the valley, that he and Telford worked together on the design and plans for construction and that Telford took charge of the actual building,

A boat floats in the air over the deep, wide valley of the Dee

with the ironmaster William Hazledine casting the ironwork and erecting it – hazardous task – on the piers.

Beyond the aqueduct, to the east, are the old Trevor transhipment basins, now a cruiser base, and the beginning of the filled-in canal to Plas Kynaston (see plan on p175 of *CWM*). To the left, by a sharp turn, is the narrow waterway that leads to Llangollen, winding its wooded way above the turbulent river.

Places Nearby
The lovely waterway from Pontcysyllte upwards past Llangollen was built as a navigable water feeder. Shallow, narrow, winding and often crowded, allow plenty of time to navigate it, and don't try to cruise above Llangollen. If you are driving, try to walk at any rate the upper part. Horse-drawn boat trips start

from Llangollen wharf, where there is also a Canal Exhibition Centre in an old warehouse. Beyond Llangollen at the Horseshoe Falls, Llantisilio, water is taken from the Dee to be passed the length of the canal to Hurleston reservoir and there made available for public supply.

29

Tyrley (Woodseaves) Cutting
Map 127, refs: 694320/700320

When I first cruised Tyrley cutting on a narrowed canal running between steep, ferny, rocky sides thick with bushes, trees hanging above, and in front an extraordinary bridge, I was, I confess, a trifle scared. Even now I find Tyrley more than impressive; it is, in the real sense of the word, awesome.

Tyrley or Woodseaves, a mile long and 90ft deep at its maximum, the greatest cutting on the canals, is part of the old Birmingham & Liverpool Junction Canal (later the Shropshire Union main line) that was built 1826–35 and engineered by Telford. Planned in the early railway age, it was modern for the times, built as level and straight as possible, with great embankments, deep cuttings and the minimum of locks. Telford's contractor, the engineer William Provis, found Tyrley cutting as awkward a job as any in his experience. The ground alternated between friable rock and clay, which tended to wash out in rain or dry out in sun, and so caused exposed rock to fall. Some rock had to be supported with walls, some to be cut back, before the cutting was safe. Muscle, men's and horses', made Tyrley in the days before mechanical aids.

The cutting can best be seen by boat: if not, then on foot along the towpath from Tyrley locks (ref: 690325). Walk up the path, following the canal as it swings first to the right and then, under a bridge, to the left again into a long, diminishing straight. The next bridge is an oddity. Why did Telford, so fond of iron bridges, build one of masonry here? And why a narrow arch and great piers carried right down to canal level and seeming to slope slightly inwards as they do so? It straddles the canal loftily, carrying the eye forward along the water as if through the eye of a huge needle.

Places Nearby
Back at Tyrley locks, let us first enjoy the nice group of brick and stone wharf buildings and the lockkeeper's snug cottage just below, all set among trees, before setting off towards the south to find more of Telford's engineering. Make for the *Wharf* inn at Shebdon (ref: 758261) where the canal crosses the road on an aqueduct, towering over the little old boatmen's pub. Up on the towpath and walking west, we are on the Shebdon embankment, a mile long and 50ft high at its greatest, with wide views.

Back to Shebdon and then left to the A519 where it crosses the canal (ref: 790242). On the towpath here, we are in the middle of the second major excavation on the canal, the 80ft-deep Grub Street cutting nearly two miles long. The bridge itself is worth looking at – high, and with a stone strut across the arch upon which stands a diminutive telegraph pole. Return now along the A519 for a few yards, then left for Norbury and through it to Norbury Junction. 'Junction' because formerly a branch canal to Shrewsbury began here – its top lock is today used as a dry-dock. Norbury is now a small canal 'place', with its maintenance yard, boatyard still using canal buildings, *Junction* inn with murals by Tony Lewery who wrote *Narrow Boat Painting* (David & Charles), and horse-drawn trip-boat.

Finally, let us return to Norbury and turn left and left again onto a by-road that runs beside the canal's greatest embankment, 60ft high and a mile long, that of Shelmore which nearly broke Telford's heart. Indeed, he died the year before Shelmore ceased to slip and settle, so that boats could pass it at last. The road cuts through the embankment to end canalside at Gnosall by the A518.

Three Junctions:
Great Haywood, Fradley, Huddlesford
Maps 127, 128

There is always something of interest at a canal junction: here are three.

Great Haywood near Stafford (ref: 995230) is at the junction of two Brindley canals, the Trent & Mersey and the Staffordshire & Worcestershire. It is one of the country's earliest canal junctions, having been operational from 1772.

From the T & M one turns into the S & W under a graceful brick roving bridge that carries the T & M's towpath over the S & W entrance. Beyond, a basin opens out, with wharf buildings to the right, now occupied by a boatyard, and a corn mill beyond. To the left are rope-worn bollards and a little toll-office with iron-framed Gothic windows. Just beyond, a single span takes the canal over the tail of the mill-race, followed by a low four-arched aqueduct over the Trent. The parapets of both are of later date, however. Then follows a short embankment before the waterway widens out into Tixall Wide, an ornamental and bird-popular lake, which is supposed to be the price the canal company had to pay for the local landowner's consent – clearly he was an early environmentalist. With luck you will spot a kingfisher here. Above the Wide stands Tixall's four-towered ruined gatehouse.

A short way south along the T & M from the junction is the sixteenth century Essex bridge, a thirteen-arched footbridge that crosses the Trent to Shugborough Park. The Museum of Staffordshire Life is housed in a stable block of Shugborough Hall, a National Trust property.

Take the A513 now and then the Fradley road to the canal; just before the crossing turn right for Fradley Junction (ref: 141140) where the Coventry Canal comes in to join the T & M. I still remember my delight as I first came to the junction from the Coventry, and saw facing me Fradley's terraced row of uneven cottages and warehouses, the *Swan* in the centre. The

An eighteenth-century roving bridge at Great Haywood; it was restored recently as a contribution to European Architectural Year

Swan is a nice pub, though crowded at weekends. Under its cellar bar runs the overflow channel joining the T & M's Middle lock above, and Junction lock below. Canal maps and other material decorate its walls. Canal-horse stables still stand, too, for the *Swan*, like many another canalside pub, put up towing horses overnight in working days. There is also a boatyard at Fradley, and a maintenance yard. The junction is a close-knit whole, in contrast to Great Haywood's more diffused pleasures.

Huddlesford (ref: 152097) was, sadly not is, a junction, for in 1954 the Wyrley & Essington Canal, which came from the Birmingham direction down a long flight of locks past Lichfield to join the Coventry Canal here, was abandoned, and now only a few hundred yards from the junction, used as moorings, are in water. But these are pretty and worth finding. A mile up the old canal is the chamber of the first rising lock, and a brick lockhouse. There is talk of restoring the Wyrley & Essington to link Huddlesford once more to the Birmingham Canal Navigations.

A cottage stands at the junction; there is a toll island that is a real reminiscence of the BCN (part of which system the W & E became) and, nearby, the *Plough*. I remember Huddlesford best for the swan. It hove itself out of the canal and waddled across the towpath, up a cottage front path between the bordering flowers, and in at the front door. I waited to see whether it would be thrown out, but no. Clearly it had stayed to lunch.

31

The Caldon Canal: Hazlehurst to Froghall
Map 118, ref: 947538 to map 119, ref: 025477

After many years of disuse, the Caldon Canal from its junction with the Trent & Mersey at Etruria in Stoke-on-Trent to Froghall was reopened in 1974. I include the last eight miles for their exceptional beauty and variety of interest. The stretch from Hazlehurst to Cheddleton can be followed by road; thence it can only be walked or cruised to Froghall, where again there is road access.

We begin then at Hazlehurst Junction, where a branch to Leek turns off, unexpectedly, to the right, and then swings to the left over the Caldon on the white-painted single arch of the Denford (or Hazlehurst) aqueduct, built in brick, with graceful moulding, corbelled balustrade and flared wing-walls. One of the few canal over canal crossings, Denford is dated 1841.

The Leek branch then winds along the hillside above the river Churnet, passes through Leek tunnel (130yds) and ends soon afterwards on a stone aqueduct over the river – the last stretch into Leek has been filled in. Just before the terminus is the Rudyard lake feeder. A three-mile walk along the path beside the water channel will take you to the long narrow reservoir among the woods and hills, or there is road access via Leek.

Meanwhile, the main line of the Caldon Canal has fallen through three picturesque locks, which are complete with bow-windowed white-painted lock cottage and iron towpath bridge. We now follow the Churnet valley. At Cheddleton there are two falling locks, the *Boat* inn – which waited long for the boats to return to it, and had its way – two water-driven mills for grinding flints for the pottery industry (open on summer weekend afternoons) and a canal shop. Beside the top lock is a plaque commemorating the canal's reopening.

Beyond, past $3\frac{1}{2}$ miles and two locks of delightful waterway which shares the steep and winding valley with the railway, is Consallforge, once a busy ironworking centre. Watch for kingfishers on the way. For the last mile to Consall the waterway uses the river bed itself. The *Black Lion* here joins *Tunnel House* (No 15) and the *Turf Hotel* (No 12) as a thoroughly isolated canal pub. But there is no public road to the *Black Lion*, only the towpath or the valley footpaths.

Consallforge

Then, after a look at precarious Consall station waiting room hanging over the canal, past ruined limekilns to another lock. (Earth movement probably caused the abandonment of the old lock chamber beside it). By it is another water-powered flint mill (now grinding sand for pottery glaze) and the unusual Cherry Eye canal bridge with its pointed arch. Then past a section of new canal replacing a length of old one that had been piped after landslips, and on to the 76yd Froghall tunnel and the canal's end among the ruins of limekilns at Froghall basin. Huge quantities of limestone were once brought here by horse tram-road and inclined plane from Caldon Low quarries three miles away. Off the basin can be found the ruined first falling lock of the canal extension to Uttoxeter, opened in 1811 and abandoned in 1847, traces of which can be found by the persevering.

32

Harecastle Tunnels
Map 118, refs: 837542/849517

Tunnels are not ideal sights to see, but there is something special about those at Harecastle. North west of Stoke-on-Trent, the long upward flight of the Cheshire locks has brought the narrow-boat Trent & Mersey Canal to Kidsgrove where, on our first canal cruise, we learned to buy oatcakes at the butcher's to fry with our bacon and sausages. Beyond, the canal, its water yellow-ed by ironstone, swings right and then back again to dive into the left-hand and larger of the two tunnel entrances beneath an impressive collection of notices. The other, Brindley's which was finished in 1775, smaller and lower, is blocked off.

The moving spirit of the Trent & Mersey company was the potter Josiah Wedgwood, a memorial tablet to whose connec-tion with the canal is by the southern portal. Its engineer was James Brindley, that brilliant, obstinate, opinionated, practical man who in 1766 agreed to build the ninety-mile long line from the Trent to the Bridgewater Canal. Near the middle, just north of the Potteries, lay Harecastle hill. This Brindley proposed to tunnel for $1\frac{1}{2}$ miles. Familiar on the Bridgewater Canal with boat tunnels carried into mines (see No 35), he began upon the first canal tunnel to be undertaken in Britain, and hit both methane and springs of water, so that in the first two years only 409yds were cut. However, he made progress, using a windmill for ventilation and an improved Newcomen engine for pumping.

Men who came to see it called it the eighth wonder of the world. Maybe it was not that but when, eleven years later, it had been completed – by his brother-in-law Hugh Henshall, for Brindley had died in 1772 – it was indeed an impressive portent of the future. A 9ft-wide narrow-boat tunnel, it was 2,880yds long without a towpath, so that boats had to be legged through by men lying on their backs on transverse boards, pushing on the tunnel sides with their feet. In making it, Brindley had struck coal. Side tunnels were therefore cut, along which small ten-ton boats used to carry out the mining output.

In time the growing two-way traffic of the tunnel could not be passed at the slow pace of the leggers, so in 1827 Telford opened a new one. Larger, it had a horse towpath. Both were now used, each for one-way traffic. In 1914 an electric tug, first hauling a battery boat, later picking up current from overhead wires, took over, and Brindley's bore was closed. The tug hauled itself, clanking and grinding and echoing, along a cable lying on the tunnel bottom. By 1954, however, boats were self-propelled, so the tug was taken off. Because Harecastle had no ventilation shafts, extractor equipment was installed in the odd structure built round the south portal to keep the tunnel clear of fumes. More recently, engineers have been removing the old towpath to enable boats to move under the centre of the tunnel and not to one side.

Harecastle has suffered much from subsidence. When I first went through, my boat had to pass under a profile hung outside, to make sure it could get beneath a dramatically low section, where I had to bend down and peer along the side of the boat to guide it. More than once the tunnel has had to be closed for treatment, and in 1974 further remedial work began.

At one point, a mine tunnel for Brindley's bore cuts across Telford's, and here the old men claim to have seen the horrid hovering spectre of Kit Crew. But even without a ghost, the echoing beat of the engine, the yellow swirling water, the dripping brickwork, the tiny point of light ahead and the other behind, the moving pool of the headlight's gleam, these are excitement enough.

Places Nearby
To the south lies Stoke-on-Trent, where at Etruria, in the middle of a curiously impressive industrial landscape, the Caldon Canal (No 31) begins. North from the tunnels, by the *Blue Bell* at Kidsgrove, the Macclesfield Canal (opened 1831) unexpectedly goes off to the left before swinging round to cross the main line (which has meanwhile started to fall by the first two Cheshire locks) by Red Bull aqueduct before disappearing north to run through great cuttings and over high embankments past Congleton and Macclesfield to Marple (No 36). One lock further down the flight is Kidsgrove maintenance yard, usually with a selection of working craft tied up.

33

Chester
Map 117, ref: 400666

Chester, with encircling city walls almost intact and two-tiered shopping streets, is itself a sight. So is the canal built in the moat beneath the walls and Northgate locks cut from the solid rock.

The Chester Canal, planned to run from the Dee via Nantwich to the Trent & Mersey at Middlewich, was to be the port of Chester's reply to the success of Manchester's Bridgewater Canal. But it wasn't. Begun in 1772 as a broad lock waterway, it had struggled to Nantwich by 1779 and there ended for lack of money to continue. Then in 1793 the Ellesmere Canal was authorised to link Mersey, Dee and Severn. One broad canal section of it, the Wirral line, ran from the Mersey at what is now Ellesmere Port to join the Chester Canal here. Both later became part of the Shropshire Union system.

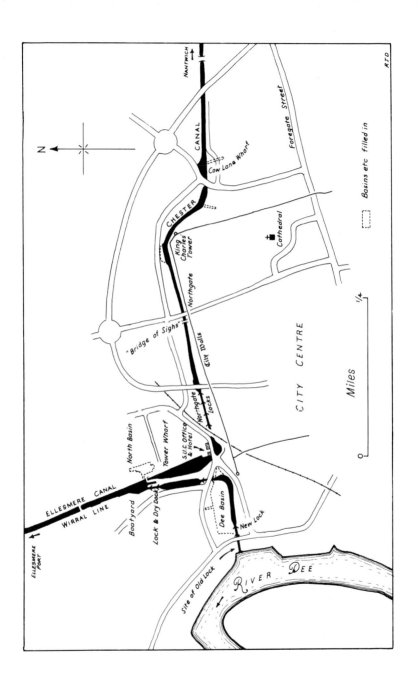

N

NANTWICH

CHESTER CANAL

Cow Lane Wharf

Foregate Street

King Charles' Tower

Cathedral

Basins etc filled in

"Bridge of Sighs"

Northgate

City Walls

CITY CENTRE

Miles

Northgate Locks

North Basin

Tower Wharf

S.U.C. Office & Hotel

ELLESMERE CANAL

WIRRAL LINE

ELLESMERE PORT

Boatyard

Lock & Dry Dock

Dee Basin

New Lock

Site of Old Lock

RIVER DEE

R.T.D.

The towpath can be reached at Hoole Lane bridge (No 123 A); coming out of the city from Foregate Street, Hoole Lane is off Boughton to the left. Hoole Lane lock is just before the bridge. We are now on the original Chester Canal, walking back towards the city. More bridges, some grain warehouses and wharves, and then the canal swings right and left to pass King Charles's Tower on' the corner of the wall and run in what was once the city moat, cut in Roman times through the red sandstone of the plant-festooned rock on which the city walls stand. Northgate bridge follows, the city's North Gate being almost above us, and beyond it a stone footbridge, the 'Bridge of Sighs', which the canal company had to build to connect Northgate Gaol to its chapel. Northgate locks open at the far end of the cutting, commanding a wonderful view across to north Wales. The chambers of this three-lock staircase are partly cut out of rock. At the top, by a wide-eaved lockhouse, there is a plaque of slate and granite to mark the Chester Canal's bicentenary in 1972. Part way down is a graceful iron-railed footbridge, while flights of steps descend each side of the lock gates.

Once there were five locks in the staircase, for the Chester Canal then fell straight to a tidal basin by the Dee, as one can see if one looks straight down from the top of the flight. Now, however, the canal swings to the right in a very sharp turn under a railway bridge. Just before the turn, on the right, is a two-storey white-painted building with a simple pediment. This was once the headquarters of the Shropshire Union Company.

Tower wharf is to the right of the turn: its hand-operated crane and brick warehouse face us, the back of the canal offices beyond, and a boatyard further down. We are in the wide, cruiser-lined basin where the Wirral line ends. Packet-boats once started from here, taking passengers to bathe in the Mersey. The wharf building next to the offices was once the Canal Hotel that catered for packet-boat passengers.

Across an iron towpath bridge and sharp left is the dry-dock, with wide-spreading slate roof. It dates from 1798, and SU boats and barges used to be built here. Three locks lead back and down to the Dee: the first close to the dry-dock; below the second a former basin has been filled in; and the last lock and

bridge were built recently to replace the old lock and the single-track swing bridge that carries New Crane Street. Only enough river water fills the approach channel to work this lock for about two hours each high tide.

Place Nearby
The harbour of the Roman city was under the modern racecourse, the Roodee. A large section of Roman quay wall can be seen from the racecourse below the city walls to the south of the county stand.

34

Anderton Lift
Map 118, ref: 647752

Anderton, to a canal enthusiast, means the glorious Victorian iron vertical lift that connects the Trent & Mersey Canal above and the Weaver Navigation below. It is best approached along the T & M towpath from the bridge at ref: 643753.

The county-owned Weaver Navigation had in the 1860s a large trade with the Potteries via the Trent & Mersey. Cargoes were physically transhipped at Anderton, where the two water-ways ran near each other, using chutes and tramways. In 1865 the Weaver's engineer, Edward Leader Williams, proposed a lift to join the two routes without loss of water to the T & M. The authorities agreed and, designed by Edwin Clark, it was opened in 1875.

With a lift of 50ft 4in, boats are carried in one of two caissons each 75ft × 15½ft × 5ft, which rise and fall within an iron framework. Each caisson, weighing 240 tons with its water, was originally supported by a 3ft diameter iron ram moving vertically in a cast-iron hydraulic press, the two presses being linked by a 5in diameter pipe. The lift's movement was started by removing

The glorious Victorian iron vertical lift at Anderton

6in of water (15 tons) from the bottom caisson. This caused the upper one to start falling, its speed being regulated by the rate of transfer of hydraulic fluid through the 5in pipe from one press to the other. When the falling caisson became partially immersed, the hydraulic pipe was closed, the upper press being then linked to a hydraulic accumulator whose power had been stored by a steam engine. When 6in below upper canal level, the rising caisson was stopped and its water restored to bring it level with the upper canal. Boats then passed out along a 162ft long three-span iron aqueduct to the Trent & Mersey. Electric power was substituted for steam in 1903, and by 1908 the hydraulic ram had been done away with. Instead J. A. Saner, now Weaver engineer, built a new framework over the lift, and provided two rows of counterbalance weights. These, helped by electric power, now work each caisson separately. In 1974–5 the lift was taken out of service for a thorough overhaul and replacement programme prior to its centenary in 1975.

Try to get a ride in a boat up and down the lift. It is quite an experience, and unique in this country.

Places Nearby
Just across the basin from the lift is Anderton depot, where some 60,000 tons a year are handled. Commercial craft can be berthed out of the river channel, and their cargoes warehoused till needed.

Move upstream into Northwich, and note the design of the first two swing bridges you come to, installed in the 1890s (refs: 657738, 657736). These and others on the Weaver are unique in Britain, built to counter the danger of their foundations subsiding due to salt extraction. The central buoyancy tank, above which the bridge swings, takes 90 per cent of the weight, so that the bridge almost floats. By a third, smaller, swing bridge beyond is a repair yard, where lock gates are made to measure by hand: it shows us a group of pleasant eighteenth-century brick buildings with an unusual classical clocktower having a cupola on pillars above the clockface. Higher up are Hunts locks (ref: 657729), the larger being 220ft × 42ft 6in. Weaver locks were given water-power operated gates a century ago, using two pelton wheels to each gate. Note the railway-type traffic signals.

Alternatively, from Anderton follow the Trent & Mersey Canal a little way towards Preston Brook to see Barnton (572yd) and Saltersford (424yd) tunnels, the one following the other. From the tree-bordered piece of canal between the two one gets a fine view of the Weaver's Saltersford locks in the valley below.

35

Barton Swing Aqueduct
Map 109, ref: 767977

It is not often that something is really unique, but the Barton swing aqueduct is: as far as I know, there is not another in the world.

Until the 1880s, boats passed by the Mersey & Irwell river navigation to Manchester. At Barton this was crossed by the Bridgewater Canal on Brindley's three-arched masonry aqueduct 38ft above the river that in 1761 had been a wonder of its time. Then came the building of the Manchester Ship Canal, much of it, as at Barton, along the course of the Mersey & Irwell. Barton aqueduct had to go, but what could replace it that would not obstruct the ship canal with its minimum clearance under bridges of 75ft, yet keep traffic moving on the Bridgewater? One idea was that it should cross by two Anderton-type vertical lifts, one each side of the ship canal, and a connecting high level aqueduct. However, by January 1884 a swing aqueduct had been decided upon. It was designed by the ship canal's engineer, Edward Leader Williams (who had earlier initiated Anderton lift). First barge over was the *Ann* of Lymm, on 21 August 1893, just before the ship canal was finished. The old aqueduct was then demolished, though an abutment can be seen.

With Anderton lift (No 34) and Foxton inclined plane (No 53), Barton swing aqueduct is a memorial to late-Victorian enterprise, when British waterway engineering rivalled that of the Continent and America. It is of wrought iron, 235ft long, 33 ft high, with a tank width of 18ft, and carries 6ft of water. When the aqueduct has to be swung, pairs of hydraulically operated gates at each end shut off the canal from the swinging section. Hydraulic machinery worked from a control tower on the central pier then swings the structure, which weighs 1,450 tons (800 tons being water) on 64 rollers, until it lies parallel to the ship canal and in the centre of its channel. When the aqueduct moves, the upward thrust of a central press takes some 900 tons of weight off the roller bearings. Once the aqueduct has been restored to its normal position, rams force U-shaped rubber-faced wedges each weighing 12 tons against each joint, and so make it watertight. Obviously, the aqueduct's success depends upon the maintenance of an exact level and the avoidance of the slightest tendency to tilt, or of the water to oscillate. Just west of it, Barton road bridge over the ship canal swings with it, being pivoted on the same island and controlled from the same tower.

Places Nearby
Below the swing aqueduct, on the ship canal, Barton locks are gay with flower beds (ref: 747966). They can be reached by car: ask at the swing bridge, or use a local street map.

At the Delph,Worsley(ref: 748006), seek the iron oxide-stained water in the silted basin which, through two small tunnels into the cliff, still visible, gave access from the original Bridgewater Canal to the Duke's coalmines. These tunnels led to many miles of underground canal on three levels, connected partly by an inclined plane (still there, but not accessible) and partly by vertical shafts. Small containers of coal were loaded onto boats within the mine; these were then brought out and towed in trains to Manchester. Beside the canal basin is the Packet House, a half-timbered building where once passenger boats started for Manchester – the embarkation steps are still there.

36

Marple
Map 109, ref: 962884

At Marple the Macclesfield Canal coming from near Harecastle

Marple: 'At the foot of the locks Benjamin Outram's Marple aqueduct spans the Goyt 100 ft above the river'

tunnels (No 32) meets the Peak Forest climbing out of Manchester towards its termini at Buxworth and Whaley Bridge. A visit offers a great aqueduct and lock flight in beautiful Peak District country.

Let us begin on the Macclesfield (opened 1831) as it enters the junction, under the lovely curves of a stone roving bridge with flat, white-painted arch. This ingenious design enabled a towing horse to change towpaths without the towrope having to be cast off. Beyond, facing us, is Top Lock House; an old boat-builders' dry-dock, reached from a short branch, is now a sunk garden in its grounds. To the right the Peak Forest continues round the hillsides at 500ft to Whaley Bridge; to the left is the first of sixteen narrow locks that fall 210ft to the aqueduct. The Peak Forest was opened in 1800, the lock flight in 1804, a tramroad being used to tranship cargoes meantime. These locks, and the canal below, were reopened in 1974 after having been unnavigable for many years.

This is all upland country, and to moor overnight at the high, wide summit shows a delight of lights scattered over the hills. The path down the flight is, I suppose, as lovely a tree-bordered summer walk as any canal in Britain offers: you will pass Posset bridge with its separate tunnel for boathorses and disused arch leading to former limekilns; the pleasant stone-built cottage at lock 9; and 'Oldknow's' warehouse.

At the foot of the locks Benjamin Outram's Marple aqueduct spans the Goyt. Masonry built, 309ft long, the centre arch is 100ft above the river. There are open roundels between the arches and the bottom of the trough, and tremendous red sandstone bases to the piers set in the river below. Because of frost during the hard winter of 1962, part of the outer face of one span collapsed; it was, however, repaired, though in reinforced concrete. Beyond the aqueduct is a stretch of walled canal where stood Rosehill tunnel (100yd) before it was opened out in the 1820s.

Places Nearby
I suggest a visit to Bugsworth (Buxworth) basin (map 110, ref: 022820), the transhipment point for limestone brought down from the Peak Forest company's Doveholes quarries by horse tramroad until 1922. Enthusiasts are clearing the basin so that its extensive industrial remains can be studied. At its greatest, Bugsworth had three basin wharves with warehouses, limekilns, stables, blacksmiths' shops, pubs, and 8,500yd of tramroad sidings. It then loaded some forty boats and 600 tons a day.

The Whaley Bridge branch of the canal (ref: 012818) gave access to the end of the thirty-three-mile-long Cromford & High Peak Railway which rose over the hills to 1,264ft and then fell to the Cromford Canal (No 51). More than one plan to build a canal over the Peak was made before this railway was opened in 1831. With nine inclined planes, the line was horse-worked until 1841, after that with locomotives. The last section closed in 1967. The stone transhipment warehouse where canal met railway still stands: from it rose the first inclined plane.

A little south west of Whaley Bridge is Toddbrook canal reservoir, and two miles east is Coombs. Both are used for sailing and fishing, and access is easy.

37

The Lune Aqueduct
Map 97, ref: 483638

There are three main types of canal aqueduct: those of masonry, those of masonry with an iron-plated channel, and those with only an iron trough. John Rennie's Lune aqueduct is, to my mind, the most impressive example of the first kind, the Avon (No 42) of the second, and Pontcysyllte (No 28) of the third. To have seen all three is to understand something of what the Canal Age meant to its contemporaries.

The Lancaster Canal was planned from Wigan northwards to Kendal. Over the Lune just north of Lancaster, in country of fields and hills, Rennie erected his great structure, five-arched, 640ft long, 62ft above the river, and opened it in 1797. Its style is plainly classical, simpler than the same engineer's Dundas aqueduct (No 10), but with the same characteristic very deep cornice. The arches are almost semicircular, massive wing-walls are gently curved and the whole length is balustraded. Each central arch has a tablet on it. That on the north side reads 'To Public Prosperity', that on the south records the names of the engineer and contractor, Alexander Stevens, and exhibits a Latin inscription which has been translated as:

> Old needs are served, far distant sites combined:
> Rivers by art to bring new wealth are joined.

One can here compare the work of engineers almost two centuries apart by looking upstream from the aqueduct to where, $\frac{3}{4}$ mile away, the M6 bridges the Lune.

Places Nearby
The pleasant walk down the towpath to Lancaster is rewarding,

'Over the Lune, in country of fields and hills, Rennie erected his great structure'

past mills to an old row of stables now converted to other purposes. A trip-boat works from here. Beyond is the ruined packet-boat house. In its flourishing days before the railways came, fast canal passenger services operated between Preston and Kendal using very light boats towed by relays of horses. Such boats were floated into the packet house and then lifted out of the water to the first floor for overhaul.

South, near Galgate (map 102, ref: 482545) is the branch to Glasson dock, opened in 1825. Here one can get onto the tow-path and walk past a large boatyard with its newly dug basin to the junction. Before turning down the branch, however, look at bridge 85 just beyond, with two roadways over it, divided longitudinally from each other.

Six broad locks run down the Conder valley to Glasson. This

was the Lancaster Canal's connection with the sea, as it still is. The sizeable lock paddles are of the unusual sliding type that one also finds on the Leeds & Liverpool Canal. The branch runs into the surprisingly big expanse of the basin, some 500yd × 400yd, surrounded by a brightly painted miscellany of pubs and other buildings. Yachts and cruisers are moored here, and an old Lancaster Canal barge has become a floating restaurant. Beyond the basin a swing bridge and lock leads to the tidal dock where coasters come up the Lune estuary. I always like to return to Glasson, for it has a welcoming air. There is a feel of the sea about it.

Further south again at the canal basin at Garstang, a Lancaster Canal Museum and Information Centre has been opened at Th'Owd Tithe Barn Restaurant (enquiries Garstang 4486).

38

Burnley Embankment
Map 103, ref: 845335/843321

When Robert Whitworth planned the Burnley embankment, I don't suppose he thought it would be called one of the seven wonders of the waterways. He was building a long level stretch of the Leeds & Liverpool Canal downwards from Barrowford locks and the Pennines to Blackburn, and reckoned that from the excavation of nearby Gannow tunnel and its southern approach cutting he could get most of the 345,000 cu yds of spoil for the great bank he intended.

The embankment is some 46ft high and ¾ mile long, neither the highest nor the longest, for Shelmore (see No 29) on the Shropshire Union main line is longer and higher. It is perhaps its extraordinary situation that makes it so impressive, running right across the town of Burnley above smoking chimneys and tall mills, while on either side stretch long views, Pendle Hill to the north west, the Yorkshire moors towards Hebden Bridge to the east.

I suggest a towpath walk for about two miles, all in Burnley, beginning at Colne Road bridge (ref: 843333). Soon the canal swings to the right in a semicircle, and after the next bridge the embankment begins, first crossing the river Brun, then over a main street, then the Calder. Soon after its end another curve to the right leads to BWB's Burnley yard, also a boatyard. More curving canal, and suddenly Gannow tunnel (559yds) opened in 1801, shows ahead. It has no towpath, steam tugs having been introduced in 1887 to speed up the slow passage by legging until self-propelled craft made them unnecessary. You can, however, make your way over the top (the path still carries a Boat Horse Lane nameplate) to see the cutting at the far end. Throughout the walk the observant eye can pick up very much of interest: details from houses, warehouses and factories built when the canal was the valley's main means of transport.

Places Nearby
I recommend taking the road to the bottom of Barrowford locks (ref: 868396). To the right are two locks and Swinden aqueduct over the Colne Water, to the left five locks in quick succession climb to the summit level. To their right is the small Barrowford reservoir, while away to the left, near enough for a climb, rises the lovely shape of Pendle Hill.

And so to Foulridge (ref: 888425). Just before you reach the village, on either side of the road stretch the canal reservoirs that feed the summit. At Foulridge make your way down through this very pleasant village to the canalside to see the eastern portal of the tunnel; nearly a mile long, it was opened in 1796. Unusually, half of it was excavated by cut and cover, ie as an open cutting afterwards arched over and filled in, because of the poor ground.

You cannot leave Foulridge without hearing of the cow that in 1912 swam the length of the tunnel, and had to be revived with brandy. And if you don't believe it, there is a photograph in the bar of the *Hole in the Wall* to prove it true.

39

Last Canal in England – the Carlisle Canal
Map 85

Ordnance maps mark, running north east out of Carlisle, a disused railway track that winds curiously compared to its brethren to north, east and south. Follow it west across Burgh Marsh to Drumburgh, and then north to Port Carlisle. Why Port Carlisle? Because this is the route of the old Carlisle Canal, opened in 1823. It lived for thirty years, and then the company built a railway along the canal bed – hence the windings and the curious appearance the bed now has, the railway formation centred within the wider canal. The waterway was $11\frac{1}{4}$ mile long, with eight locks and no overbridges – a substantial affair that brought 100-ton sailing craft to the city and ran passenger boats to connect at Port Carlisle with steamers to Liverpool.

The old yard and basin in Carlisle is at ref: 392559 off the B5307 to the right just after it has left the A595. Canal Street is opposite its entrance, the *Jovial Sailor* beside it. As one turns into it, the former Newcastle & Carlisle Railway's canal branch track is on the left running to the basin and former wharves beyond.

Facing the yard entrance when I first came here was a fine four-storey brick warehouse dated 1821. Sadly it was demolished in 1974. The canal basin was beyond it. To the right is a row of what seem to be single-storey stores. In fact, these coal and lime vaults are much deeper, there being road access from below. Coal, therefore, could be unloaded at the wharf into the stores and later withdrawn by cart. On the far side and to the left of the basin is the little 1832 Custom House that owed its business to the canal.

Between Carlisle and Port Carlisle a swingbridge keeper's cottage can be seen at Wormanby at ref: 344589; east of a lock cottage at ref: 344590, a short stretch of canal not used for the railway is still watered. Just beyond Burgh by Sands, a lock-keeper's house and a bollard stand by the road to Longburgh at ref: 307592.

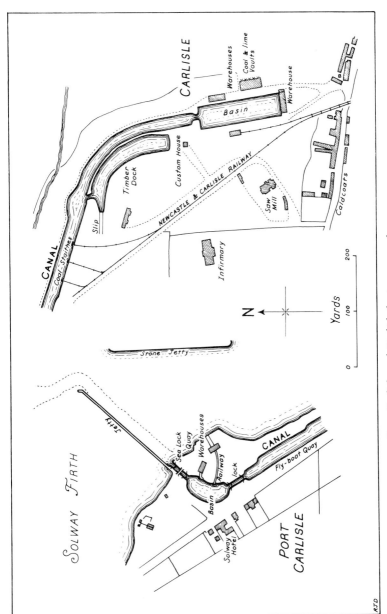

Port Carlisle and Carlisle basin as once they were

At Port Carlisle, let us find Solway House, a good-looking two-storey building with a pillared porch, once the Solway Hotel, where passengers put up while transferring from canal packet-boats to the steamers. If we stand with our backs to it and look to our right over the former railway, we can imagine the fly-boat quay where canal passengers landed. A little nearer, parallel to the road, is the canal's last lock, with three bollards beyond it, then a wide curving basin now empty and grass-grown, and then ahead and in line with our eyes, the canal's sea-lock, still with its masonry entrance walls. Beyond on its left-hand side, some timbers mark the wooden jetty where steamers once moored. The wharves were to the right of the sea-lock: two warehouses stood there and a little goods tramway ran from the basin through one warehouse to the wharves. Both are now houses. Wharves and steamer jetty were protected by a stone jetty opposite the wooden one, backed by a large mound, of which traces can be seen. To our left is the railway station and beyond, the last house in the row, the plain red sandstone building that was once the *Steam Packet Inn*. Try to visit Port Carlisle at high water springs: the canal basin fills with water and for a moment recreates the past.

In 1835 it took Sir George Head two hours from Carlisle to here, past the canal's six other locks, in the *Arrow*. She was pulled by two stout horses at 10mph, a postilion on the hindmost horse driving the other. She carried forty people and a great deal of luggage and yet drew only twelve inches of water.

We have met the tides elsewhere in this book. But here at Port Carlisle, the openness of the Solway Firth seems more immediate, the union of canal and sea more dramatic. Over there is Scotland: this is the last canal in England.

40

Crinan
Map 55, ref: 789944

I always think of Crinan as the canal by the sea. Other canals

Crinan: 'This small place nestling beneath the cliff'

offer land views, of hills, rivers, valleys, villages or towns. But as I came down the Crinan Canal on a sunny day, past the narrow Bellanoch section where the waterway squeezes between the cliffs and the sea, and on towards Crinan, I looked across Loch Crinan to the green and purple heights behind Duntrune Castle, while to the left the Sound of Jura spread silent and shining towards Scarba. Faintly came the roar of the Corryvreckan whirlpool between Scarba and Jura.

The Crinan Canal winds round the narrow strip of flat land between Loch Crinan and the hills to this small place nestling beneath the cliff. It has a mooring basin, a canal lock, a turning basin giving on to a small dock (the old sea-lock before reconstruction in 1930–32), and then the sea-lock. One or two buildings stand beside the lock, and on the point is the Crinan Hotel. A lighthouse, a handful of buildings beside the sea, and that is Crinan. The old steam trading puffers have gone; yachts now use the canal to cross the peninsula of Kintyre, and fill the Crinan basins.

Lighthouses on canals are curiosities. There is one at Ardrishaig at the other end of this canal, and others on the Caledonian. The Carlisle Canal once had one, and so did Ellesmere Port on the Shropshire Union.

The Crinan Canal is nine miles long from Crinan to Ardrishaig on Loch Gilp. Fully opened in 1809 with fifteen locks, it was built mainly as a philanthropic exercise to improve communications with the western Highlands and islands by cutting off the long detour round the Mull of Kintyre, and so cheapen carriage. However, philanthropy, even helped by the state, was not able to spend enough on the canal. John Rennie had to make it less deep than had been intended, and to give it a very short summit level, only ⅝ mile long, fed by eight linked reservoirs, instead of cutting it right through at a lower level.

From 1819, when Henry Bell's pioneer *Comet* began running between Glasgow and Fort William by way of the canal, steamer services used it, in 1825 these being extended through the Caledonian Canal also to Inverness, with Crinan as an overnight stop. Later, horse-drawn packet- or track-boats, pulled at 8–10 mph, also worked on the local run between Crinan and Ardrishaig: it was on the track-boat *Sunbeam* that Queen Victoria passed through in August 1847. These were later replaced by the little steamer *Linnet*, which shuttled the length of the canal till passenger services ended in 1929. Her photograph is in the public bar of the *Royal Hotel* at Ardrishaig, and a different one in the cocktail bar of the *Argyll Arms*.

Places Nearby
The whole length of the canal towpath to Ardrishaig is well worth walking for its beauty and variety, past Dunardry (note the odd roller bridge over lock 11), Cairnbaan with its hotel, and Lochgilphead to Ardrishaig, the village where, guarded by another lighthouse and a small harbour wall, the canal enters Loch Gilp.

Fort Augustus
Map 34, ref: 377092

The whole Caledonian Canal is a 'sight'. A glance at a relief map of Scotland shows the Great Glen running diagonally through the Highlands from Loch Linnhe north east to the Moray Firth. Three big lochs lie along the Glen, Lochy, Oich and Ness, and a small one, Dochfour. To connect them to each other and the sea at either end, the state built the Caledonian Canal, constructed by Telford with Jessop as consultant and opened in 1822 after nineteen years' work. Only aerial photographs can really convey the grandeur of the Great Glen, or of the canal that threads through it. Robert Southey, poet laureate, commemorated it in 1829:

> . . . in days to come
> Fitly shall this great British work be named
> With whatsoe'er of most magnificence,
> For public use, Rome in her plenitude
> Of power effected . . .

I have chosen Fort Augustus, but in the hope that readers will explore the whole canal. This little town, almost in the centre of the Glen, stands where the canal coming from Loch Oich reaches a point where Loch Ness opens out ahead, stretching beautiful but a little frightening between its mountains. It drops by five staircase locks through the town to enter Loch Ness beside Fort Augustus abbey, some houses for canal staff, and a lighthouse. The Caledonian is a small ship canal taking craft 160ft × 36ft. Nowadays not many ships pass through, but a picnic by the locks usually yields a yacht or a fishing boat being worked, not by the punishing old capstans, but by powered operation of the gates.

The Great Glen exhibition helps one to understand the physical background to this part of Scotland's history and why Fort Augustus stands where it does. Housed in old canal workshop buildings, it is usually open from April to September, and includes a Caledonian Canal section.

To get the best view of Fort Augustus, take the old road to Inverness (General Wade's military road) on the south-eastern side of Loch Ness through Foyers and Dores. It hardly needs me to suggest that, allowing hope to triumph over experience, you should look for the Loch Ness monster (or monsters, for a local leaflet says that 'obviously there must be a family of them'). In doing so it will become clear that there is a lot of water in the loch, twenty-four miles long, about a mile wide, and around 820ft maximum depth. You can look from the road, or from the water aboard the *Scot II*, which between May and October sails from the top of Muirtown locks, Inverness, to Urquhart Bay, about half way along Loch Ness, and back (no landing). Enquiries, Inverness 33140.

If possible, visit Banavie beneath Ben Nevis at the Fort William end of the canal, where the line from Loch Lochy drops through eight locks to the last short stretch before the sea-lock at Corpach. These locks are nicknamed 'Neptune's Staircase': an impressive sight they are as one stands below and looks up. By far the biggest staircase flight in Britain, it can be matched only at the eight-lock Béziers staircase in southern France, or recalled by the seven-lock flight at Berg on the Göta Canal in Sweden, for there Telford was consultant, and used his Caledonian Canal drawings as basis for the Göta's locks.

As one descends the flight, the original lockkeeper's house is on the right-hand side: its bow front gave a good view either way. To the left are the station buildings of the Banavie branch line, built to provide a connection between the canal and the West Highland Railway.

42

The Union Canal Aqueducts
Maps 66, 65

For every thousand people who have seen Pontcysyllte aqueduct, there may be one who has seen Slateford, Almond and Avon. Yet Avon is the second biggest in Britain, one of three great

The Avon Aqueduct

structures on the Edinburgh & Glasgow Union Canal.

The Union, $31\frac{1}{2}$ miles long, was built in 1817–22 to link with the older Forth & Clyde at Falkirk to provide a through water route between Edinburgh and Glasgow. Mainly a carrier of coal towards Edinburgh, the canal also had a frequent service between the two cities of fast passenger boats drawn by galloping horses.

From the Edinburgh end, we come first to Slateford Aqueduct (ref: 221708) over the Water of Leith, 75ft high and 500ft long with eight arches. Telford described it as 'superior perhaps to any aqueduct in the Kingdom'. Then on past the canalside *Bridge Inn* at Ratho, which is decorated with old canal posters and prints (the restaurant boat *The Pride of the Union* cruises from here, enquiries Ratho 320) to the five-arched aqueduct (ref: 104707) spanning Almond's steep wooded banks. At 420ft long, it is the shortest of the three, but is 76ft high. At its eastern end a feeder comes in, in itself an engineering feat. This can be followed along the valley side to its own aqueduct over the Almond – a nature trail covers most of it.

At ref: 976758 in Woodcockdale, with fine canal stables from passenger boat days and, alongside the towpath next to a half-mile stone, an inscribed stone marking the boundary between two passenger stages. Beyond (ref: 967758) is the greatest of the aqueducts, that over the Avon. This astonishing structure with its twelve arches, each 50ft span, is 810ft long, 86ft high, and 23ft 8in wide. Let us see it with the eyes of canal passengers of 1823:

This noble edifice, which, for magnificence, is scarcely equalled in Europe, consists of twelve arches, is nearly 900ft in length and 85 in height. When from the top of this bridge they look down upon the stream beneath, with the cottages, trees and cornfields, they are struck with their diminished appearance. . . It is not the grandeur of the work alone which the passenger surveys with pleasure. The woody glens, the rugged heights, and the beautiful Alpine scenery around, must raise sensations of pleasure in every feeling heart.

Thomas Telford advised Baird, the Union Canal's engineer, on the building of these aqueducts. All three have a family resemblance: stone-built, with iron troughs 13ft wide and 6ft deep, and iron railings on either side. The strongly emphasised vertical lines of the piers are continued as pilasters up to canal level. They are also first cousins to Chirk aqueduct on the Llangollen Canal; indeed, their iron plates were probably cast by Hazledine at Plas Kynaston near Pontcysyllte.

Places Nearby
Beyond the Avon aqueduct is the former Slamannan Railway coal basin, 150ft square. It was built to enable Monklands coal to be transferred from the railway (it had come down a 1 in 23 inclined plane, operated by a stationary steam engine) to the canal to be taken to Edinburgh. The Slamannan survived until 1930.

Five miles further west, at Glen village, is Falkirk (Callendar Hill) tunnel, 696yds long, and with a towpath, the only one still open in Scotland, its portals squat and low beneath the weight of their little hill. An exceptionally high road bridge spanning the canal near its eastern end has a face cut on each side, one to welcome the rising sun, one to mourn its setting. Some call it the Laughin' and Greetin' bridge. Nothing remains of the eleven locks that took the canal down to the Forth & Clyde at Falkirk, except, beside the former junction, the *Union Inn*. The former name of Port Downie is recalled on a building of the nearby starch works.

In the opposite direction, at Lower Gilmore Place canal crossing in Edinburgh, is a late-nineteenth-century vertical lift bridge with a hugely substantial iron framework. Originally at the Fountainbridge crossing, it was moved here in 1913, when the section of canal beyond was filled in. It was worked by a steam engine until about 1922, then by electric power until 1928 when it ceased operation.

43

Ripon
Map 99, ref: 315708

The Ripon Canal, over two centuries old, is no longer navigable through to the city, though plans to reopen it may be realised before long. Yet Ripon is a waterway sight to see (apart, that is, from the cathedral, nearby Fountains abbey, and the delightful town itself), in general because it is the most northerly point on England's east side to which regular navigation reached, in particular because of the interesting and I think unique layout of the old canal basin which, though abandoned, is still supplied with water from the river Skell.

The white-painted *Navigation* inn stands at the head of the basin; below, past the wharf gateposts, one with a curious iron ornament on it, and a derelict wharfinger's house, are warehouses with red-tiled roofs. Then, on the left side of the canal looking back from the *Navigation*, down Bondgate Green, a row of single-storey buildings begins, one beside the wharf gate having a pleasant curved wall. Beyond these runs a tree-shaded wall pierced with sets of double gates, each one an entrance to a separate yard where once coal was landed, each formerly complete with wharf space alongside the canal, stacking area, and a small brick and tile office building by the gate.

Navigation of the canal now ends at Littlethorpe, lower of the two derelict locks outside Ripon, where the Ripon Boat Club that has done so much for the canal has its moorings. A bridge at ref: 327694 gives access to the canal just below this point. At Oxclose, $1\frac{1}{4}$ miles below, the Ripon Canal enters the river Ure which, below its confluence with the Swale below Boroughbridge lower down, becomes the Yorkshire Ouse.

Places Nearby
I suggest a visit to the first Ure lock below Oxclose, at Westwick (ref: 355667). Some think the Wey in Surrey is England's prettiest river navigation, others have their favourites, but I choose this remotely rural Ure. You will see what I mean at

Westwick lock. A trip-boat runs from Newby Park (open to the public) above it, should you like to sample the river. The ground paddles here and below at Milby lock are not, as is usual, set on the inside of the approach walls to the upper gates, but on their front faces.

When I last walked down the towpath of the Milby Cut from Boroughbridge (ref: 396672), barges were loading sand and gravel at a wharf above Milby lock – maybe they still do.

The river Swale joins the Ure below Milby. BWB's navigation ends at Swale Nab: thence for some miles the Linton Lock Commissioners are responsible before giving way to York Corporation. Linton lock itself (map 100, ref: 499602) is a strange place. A big lock, one of only two on the Yorkshire Ouse, a great weir, a stranded barge, a red-tiled lockhouse where one can now buy refreshments, the disused building of a small hydro-electric power station that once generated electricity for York, Linton lock is now maintained and financed largely by the Linton Lock Supporters' Club, who do indeed support the willing but impecunious Commissioners. Remote Linton, a lock in the middle of nowhere, has been a piece of history stranded out of its time. But not now. The increase in pleasure cruising, the help of the Waterways Recovery Group and others, are changing that. For history runs not only back, but forwards also, and old things are made new.

44

Three Basins: Driffield, Leven, Beverley
Map 107

The tidal river Hull runs northwards from the city on the Humber to three canals that branch from its stream – the Driffield Navigation, the Leven Canal, and Beverley Beck – the last still used by motor barges, the others disused. All three have terminal basins well worth visiting.

The canal to Driffield was opened in 1770. It remained in trading use till 1944, has never been abandoned and, one hopes, looks forward to restoration. From Brigham downwards, pleasure craft use it now. I suggest an approach to Driffield by the B1249 from Beeford on the A165: the road parallels the upper part of the canal and its parent, the river Hull. There is a disused staircase pair of locks at Snakeholme (ref: 067556), a single lock at Wansford (ref: 062562) and another at Whinhill (ref: 051568), the last two easily accessible. They were built to take sailing keels and sloops some 61ft × 14ft, carrying about 80 tons, standard craft on all the local waterways. At Wansford lock – and elsewhere – one can see paddle-gear similar to that on the Calder & Hebble (see No 47), gearing being turned by a hand-spike. A keel's anchor roller was operated like this, and probably originated the method.

Driffield welcomed me to as pleasant and nicely kept a little canal terminal as any in England. The basin ends against a street wall, from beneath which flows its feeder stream. On either side are red-brick grain warehouses, one still used as such, the others beautifully converted to flats, an example of how to do it. There are two hand-worked cranes and, further along, this notice on a low maintenance building by the public wharf:

> Whereas great damage has been done to this canal by persons letting off the water, and by the watermen opening the sluices of one gate before the others have been closed and entering the locks and bridges without lessening their speed, *Strict watch* will be kept for the future, and any person found acting as above will be fined the full amount authorised by act of Parliament.

A nice picture of the rush of modern life at Driffield fifty years ago. Some 300yds further on is Driffield lock, which maintains the water level of the basin.

The Leven Canal runs almost straight from the river to Leven on the A165. Built privately in the 1800s by the Bethell family, it only recently left their hands. It was closed in 1935. A path on the south side of the *New Inn* leads to the towpath, whence one can see the basin (ref: 107449). On each side are warehouses, one dated 1825: because of land movement they have been lowered a storey and reroofed. Its back to the end of the basin, facing the road, is a pleasant large house that may once have been that of the canal manager. There is talk of canal restoration: if so, the sadly unkempt basin may flourish once more.

Beverley Beck is ¾ mile long, once a natural stream that ran into the Hull river, later a canalisation. As a navigation it is very old, being certainly in use by 1344. Today, controlled as it always has been by the town of Beverley, it is still commercially used by motor barges of about 80 tons which come upriver from Hull and pass through Grovehill lock at the Beck's entrance to reach its wharves. Its unobtrusive termination among the old town streets is at ref: 045393. Nearby is the *Sloop*, the *Mariners Arms*, and the mooring of the Humber Keel Society's *Comrade*: with their help let us reflect upon the longevity of inland water transport, which for more than six centuries has carried cargoes to and from historic Beverley.

45

Selby
Map 105, ref: 623323

Selby is a flourishing small port on the Yorkshire Ouse, which can show a medieval warehouse as evidence of its antiquity. There, also, the two-centuries-old Selby Canal comes in from the Aire.

The Ouse extends from the Humber upwards past Goole and Selby to the end of the tide run at Naburn locks, then on past York. It was used by the Romans to supply their garrison at York, and may well have been in use for transport ever since. Selby is accessible not only for inland waterway craft, but for seagoing ships, British and foreign.

A little above the tollbridge the river curves sharply round to the east. On the outside of the curve Selby Dam, a former millstream, comes in; in medieval times its mouth was used as an anchorage. Below it, on the far side of Ideal Mills, lies the remains of Abbot's Staith, notably a building (ref: 616326) now used as garages in which a fair amount of Norman work survives.

This was once part of a sizeable warehouse, probably used to store materials brought by water for the maintenance of Selby abbey: probably also a place to store tithes paid in kind. Materials recently found during the building of a new wharf for Ideal Mills may have been sections of the old staith.

Beside Abbot's Staith are flour mills, and a little higher up the river, round the bend, oil and cake mills. Both have a considerable trade by water. To reach their wharves, ships have to pass two swing bridges, first the railway bridge with its high-perched control tower, then the road tollbridge. Try to visit Selby towards the top of the tide, and you may see the bridges swung, or be able to watch a captain's skill in holding his vessel waiting stationary on the tide.

Below the railway bridge and Ousegate river wharves, the Selby Canal enters through a river lock – note the ratchet gear for opening the gates. This is one of Britain's oldest canals, having been engineered by the young William Jessop on behalf of the Aire & Calder company and opened in 1778 to by-pass the difficult winding lower Aire. Nearly fifty years later this in turn was by-passed by the canal that now runs from the Aire at Ferrybridge to Goole. Beside Selby canal lock is a new lockhouse; above it a small basin, tree-lined on the far side, is usually full of seagoing cruisers and converted barges. Downriver from the canal lock are more wharves and a shipyard.

Places Nearby
I suggest a drive to the south. Take the A63 and then the A19, and at the first crossroads turn left for Brayton. You will soon cross the Selby Canal (ref: 611303) on one of the three remaining of Jessop's original bridges. It has a slightly elliptical arch, and the stone work is carried right back at each side to form part of the approach ramps. Back to the A19, turn left, and then continue on past the canalside *Anchor* inn at Burn bridge to the next crossroads. Continue over the Aire bridge, park, and walk a short way downstream to disused Haddlesey lock (ref: 581259). Not needed once the lower Aire had been formally abandoned, it may be restored to allow maintenance boats to reach the back of the nearby weir.

Then return over the bridge and first left. After $\frac{1}{2}$ mile the road crosses the Selby Canal above Haddlesey flood-lock (ref 571264), where the canal enters the Aire. Normally the river, held up by the weir we saw by the disused Haddlesey lock, makes a level with the canal and the gates remain open. In flood-times, however, craft can lock *down* from the river into the canal – hence taller gates at the lock's river end.

46

Bingley Five-Rise
Map 104, ref: 107391

I suppose one never ceases to be astonished at Bingley Five-rise, however many times one sees it. The pattern of lock-gates and white-railed footbridges marching steeply down, the canal curving between rows of trees, Bingley's mills behind, the hills beyond: one can look and look – especially if one is not in a boat, trying to remember the lock working instructions.

A five-rise is a series of five locks built in a single structure, the bottom gates of each being also the top gates of the next below. Therefore the fall is exceptionally steep. Staircase locks or risers were cheap to build and especially convenient on a crowded site or where the land fell sharply away. But they delayed traffic because passing on a staircase is impossible for full-width craft, and were expensive in water. Later engineers like Jessop and Rennie seldom built staircases, but John Longbotham, who planned and built this part of the Leeds & Liverpool, was of an earlier school.

The canal, $127\frac{1}{4}$ miles long, has come from Liverpool by Wigan and Burnley (No 38), then through Foulridge tunnel and, winding down the Aire valley, past Skipton to reach Bingley on its way to Leeds. The locks are broad, but shorter than in the south, taking boats 62ft long.

Between Wigan and Gargrave (above Skipton), the canal was built by later engineers who used no risers. But between Bingley and Leeds Longbotham let himself go. There is a three-rise

Bingley Five-rise: 'The pattern of lock-gates and white-railed footbridges, the hills beyond'

lower down in Bingley (locks 22–24), and three others below, Field (16–18), Newlay (11–13) and Forge (8–10), and three staircase pairs, Dowley Gap (20–21), Dobson (14–15) and Oddy (4–5). Nowhere else in England are so many staircases concentrated within sixteen miles of canal. Bingley Five-Rise itself, over 59ft high, stone-built and solid, was opened in March 1774. The bells of Bingley rang, the militia fired their guns, a band played, and the many watchers showed 'amazement and delight' as five loaded boats worked down through the five locks in twenty-nine minutes. Watchers still do, though cruisers are now the main traffic.

Places Nearby

Towards Leeds, Bingley Three-Rise is only a few hundred yards down the towpath. Rather over a mile further, just past Dowley Gap staircase pair, the unpretentious Dowley Gap masonry aqueduct takes the canal over the Aire. Beyond, past a woody cutting and not strictly a canal sight, the model village of Saltaire, built by Sir Titus Salt in the 1850s to take his workers and his mill out of Bradford, is an example of what a philanthropic and energetic Victorian industrialist could achieve by his own initiative. Across the canal from it is a pleasant park.

The opposite way, a long level pound leads to Skipton, one of my favourite small towns, its broad High Street ended by the castle, its little ginnels or side lanes leading to all sorts of oddities. The canal wharf is central, one former warehouse now a sports outfitters, the other a pub, the *Barge*. Then walk up the half-mile Springs branch, built by Lord Thanet of Skipton castle to provide his quarries with transport. It creeps through Skipton past the *New Ship*, past Higher Mill next to it, a restored water-driven working corn mill, under the steep-sided towering rock upon which the castle is built, to end where chutes once discharged limestone into waiting boats.

47

Sowerby Bridge
Map 104, ref: 060236

Of all the surviving canal basins, I myself turn back again and again to Sowerby Bridge. Set in hills and rough north country scenery, its scale and simple grandeur make a strong impression. When I first knew its tall stone warehouses with their dim, timbered interiors and its cobbled yards, it was suspended between the old life of carrying that had ended, and the new one of cruising not yet begun. The yards were grass-grown, the warehouses empty. But not now, for new life is returning to Sowerby; it is busy with boats and the spacious old buildings keep their working dignity. And yet the old lingers – and so I recommend a visit.

Sowerby Bridge basin began as the terminus of the Calder & Hebble coming from Wakefield, the river navigation with the steepest gradient in Britain. John Smeaton completed the canalisation in 1770, after the works had been damaged by floods. In 1798 the first section of the Rochdale, William Jessop's trans-Pennine canal, was opened from Sowerby upwards, then the whole canal in 1804 to Manchester. Sowerby Bridge now became a transhipment point, for the Rochdale took bigger barges than the C & H. The Rochdale's old line lies on the far side of the wharves, ending in a derelict lock. It was abandoned in 1952.

The proposed transformation of the basins includes a boatyard, waterways museum, restaurant and canalside walk; already, in one building which has a covered wet-dock, short narrow boats are being built for cruising.

Places Nearby
Let us start at the *Calder and Hebble* pub on the A6026 at Salterhebble (ref. 097224). Just west of the road bridge is the lowest of the three Salterhebble locks, with an electrically operated guillotine bottom gate, put in when road widening made it impossible to work ordinary gates. Above it is the small aqueduct Brindley built over the Hebble brook. Brought in as engineer for

a short time, he built a staircase of three here, but they were soon replaced by three single locks. A pleasant single-storey lockhouse stands by the topmost one. The paddle-gear on C & H locks is odd. Instead of using a windlass to raise the paddlebars, one engages a wooden lever or handspike in slots in a small drum, and levers away notch by notch.

A branch runs north at this point, bordering the Hebble stream. By the old wharf, dry-dock and two-storey depot house a little way up, the original navigation branch ended in 1767, before the extension to Sowerby Bridge. In 1828 a flight of fourteen locks took a branch canal from here up into Halifax, a steam pump raising the necessary water. The branch was abandoned in 1942, and has left few traces.

In the other direction from Sowerby Bridge, the bed of the Rochdale Canal has been filled in under the main road outside the basin, and on the far side it begins again, watered and easily walkable. Were I the king of all canal restorers, I would command its restoration next after that glory of the south, the Kennet & Avon. Walk, I suggest, as far as you can, and you will see why (you can get a train back on the parallel railway), if possible as far as the nice aqueduct over the Calder at Hebden Bridge (map 103). The canal winds up the valley, the great hills above, sloping fields and woods below, old industrial buildings and small wharves along the line, past the little Sowerby tunnel – really an enlarged bridge – Luddenden Foot wharf ($2\frac{1}{2}$ miles) and Mytholmroyd wharf (4 miles), into the stone country, into the Pennines.

48

Stanley Ferry Aqueduct
Map 104, ref: 356230

The Aire & Calder navigation originally followed the Calder river line. The trade expansion of the 1820s stimulated modernisation: less winding river, fewer locks, more straight and modern canal. The new line had to be carried over the old river, and

Stanley Ferry aqueduct did this when it was opened in 1839. The engineer was George Leather.

The aqueduct is a striking sight in a lonely, wide countryside. Two parallel cast-iron arches each weighing 101 tons and with a 165ft span leap the river, these being tied together with lattice work. From each arch fall 35 suspension rods which support beams holding the cast-iron trough. These rods pass down the sides of the trough through hollow iron Greek doric columns that are purely decorative, while at each corner of the aqueduct, hiding the abutments, are little doric temple facades with cornice and tympanum. Currently, because it is being used by much greater beamed craft than those for which it was designed, its condition is such that BWB are considering building a new one alongside and realigning the canal.

Floods are always a threat, for the Calder is that kind of river, as Smeaton had found when making it navigable above Wakefield. Soon after the aqueduct had been opened, indeed, a flood took the river water right over and into the trough. Even now, as a visit will show, a great semicircular barrier on the upstream side protects the structure from debris.

Just below the aqueduct is a repair yard, with its moored maintenance craft. Above, on the same side as the yard, is the former Stanley Ferry or Lofthouse basin, once the terminus of the Aire & Calder's own 3ft 4in gauge Stanley Railway which latterly ran from Lofthouse colliery. This did not reopen after the General Strike of 1926, but until recently the basin continued in use for handling coal, and later oil and grain.

Places Nearby

At ref: 353244, down a lane off the A642, stands a long row of stone buildings that was once Lake Lock depot. A smallholding has been cultivated on the land and the sloping site is attractive and friendly. It was opened in 1802 mainly to build and maintain the company's carrying craft (for original layout of area, see *CYNEE*, p126). After the opening of the new line via Stanley Ferry, work was transferred to Goole, but BWB still own the site.

At Castleford (map 105) the navigation past Stanley Ferry joins that from Leeds at ref: 424263; access is off the A656. At the junction the downstream navigation channel leaves the Aire through Castleford Flood lock, normally kept open, and enters a canal stretch. Traffic lights control the entrance, because of the sharp curve round from the Leeds line. The front of the tollhouse at the junction is typical of those built in the 1830s – brick single-storey, with heavy pilasters each side of the doorway.

On either side of the cut you will probably see compartment boats, also called pans or Tom Puddings. These are floating containers each holding up to forty tons, usually of coal, built to be coupled closely together. The first sight of a train of them, snaking down the canal, is a guaranteed surprise. Up to nineteen can be towed by a tug and passed through the longer locks in one operation. Here, too, one can usually see the modern 160-ton compartment boats that are pushed by a dumpy black and white tug in trains of three to Ferrybridge 'C' power station. The big Bulholme lock lies at the other end of the Castleford cut, its gates power-operated from a raised control cabin, its lockhouse on stilts out of the way of floods. Below the lock the cut rejoins the Aire to run down to Ferrybridge.

49

The S & SY: Doncaster to Sheffield
Map 111

The Sheffield & South Yorkshire Navigation offers us both old and new, from flourishing Rotherham depot to a canal tunnel disused for a century, a towpath walk through a barge maintenance yard, and historic Sheffield basin.

Let us begin at Doncaster wharf (ref: 575037; it is next to a prominent grain silo, and near the church) where compartment boats will probably be loading coal from road vehicles. A little higher up, curiously secretive, a web of bridge girders above it, is Doncaster lock (ref: 569036), 215ft long and 18ft 4in wide, an older lock than Long Sandall a little lower down at ref: 602067, the same in length, but narrower. It is able, however, to take three large 140-ton compartment boats and their push-tug. Not far above the lock a power station grab will be unloading coal barges. The South Yorkshire Industrial Museum at Cusworth Hall (tel: Doncaster 61842) is less than two miles away, off the A638 at ref: 547039. The whole museum is well worth a visit, the waterways room especially.

The A630 and then A6023, with a left fork after Mexborough, leads to Swinton, where the road crosses the old Dearne & Dove Canal above the locks at ref: 463992. A walk down the locks towards the S & SY main line takes one through the boatyard of E.V. Waddington Ltd; the firm started barge building 200 years ago. This is a barge maintenance yard for their carrying fleet of 90-ton steel barges, an attractive place of ordered disarray. Upwards from the locks, the short canal spur now ends beside a glassworks. But walk along the towpath under the railway bridge, then right, and the former canal bed will be seen beside the disused rail track. This however was a diverted cut made when the railway was built. More to the left the original route of the canal can be made out, and diligent scrambling will find the former Ardwick tunnel, 472yds long, built by cut-and-cover.

At ref: 425926 is Rotherham depot. Its first stage completed in 1962, it has grown to be a considerable warehousing complex, modern and efficient with over 68,000 sq ft of warehouse space.

Given Tinsley's road maze, it might be better to get on to the towpath again above Tinsley locks, off the A6102 at ref: 388893. The eleven locks are solid, workmanlike affairs that have survived a century and a half of use by keels, Sheffield-sized barges and now pleasure cruisers seeking moorings in Sheffield basin. There used to be twelve, but in 1963 two were thrown into one for the building of a railway bridge: the new one, unusually, has a concrete chamber. At the top of the flight, which falls 70ft, the view ahead is extraordinary. First the locks drop steeply neighbouring great steelworks, then ease, until they end just beyond the shadow of the double-decked road viaduct that carries both the M1 and another road. By the canal's junction with the Don, three locks above Rotherham depot, a brick building houses two diesel pumps that can lift some 2,500gpm of water back to the top of the flight.

The basin (ref: 359878) was the original end of the Sheffield Canal of 1819: some buildings date from then, others from early this century. As one enters from Exchange Street the basin road curves to the right past former offices and cottages on the left. To the right is the original terminal warehouse in red brick, a wet-dock, and the canal company's former headquarters. Further on, another warehouse straddles the basin; once its trapdoors enabled goods to be lifted direct from craft lying below. Further on again, a third extends high and wide along the length of the basin on the far side, while to our left railway lines once ran for canal-rail interchange. Disused now by commercial craft, the basin is too good to lose: there are plans to make it into an industrial museum.

Since 1966 the BWB has been trying to persuade the government to finance the enlargement of the S & SY to Rotherham. It may be, therefore, that readers will find engineering works going on along the line – I hope so.

50

The Glory-hole at Lincoln
Map 121, ref: 974712

Our waterway sight in Lincoln is the Glory-hole, and High Bridge above it in the middle of the city. The Glory-hole itself is the single, heavily vaulted 22ft arch over the navigable river Witham; it was built in the twelfth century to carry High Street, now a pedestrian area. Above it on the east side of the bridge, sixteenth-century half-timbered and gabled shops look down the line of water. The west side is open, with an extension where you can sit to watch the swans, the boats and the scene.

From street level, worn steps take one down to the towpath and east to astonishing Brayford Pool. A sheet of water at the city's centre as big as this is totally unexpected. The Romans probably made it from a natural depression, for we are now where Roman inland waterway craft once worked. The Caerdyke, a Roman artificial navigable drain, itself with branch canals, ran from near Cambridge (No 58) round the edge of the Fens to join the Witham south of Lincoln. The Witham in turn joins the Fossdyke here at Brayford Pool. The Fossdyke, another Roman work, now enlarged to a sizeable canal, runs on to join the Trent at Torksey. Along Caerdyke and Fossdyke corn was carried to Brough-on-Humber and York for the garrisons of the north, and coal brought back. A few years ago commercial barges ceased to use Brayford Pool: now it is full of pleasure craft and people doing things on boats, while round its edge a few old waterside buildings remain among the new construction.

Walk west now from High Bridge, still in the busy city, past the swans, the moored boats, the fishermen and the medieval *Green Dragon* inn to a stretch of the Witham lined with trees, warehouses and works. Stamp End lock is there, with an electrically powered, vertically rising top gate dated 1950, and lower mitre gates. Just above the top gate an elderly rolling bridge seems to be in retirement. On the far side of the railway bridge below the lock a large vertically rising road bridge, also electrically powered, lies low across the water. As I waited hopefully, a cruiser came round the corner and blew for the bridge. Gratified,

The Glory-hole at Lincoln on the Witham

I watched the heavy structure rise. From here the Witham runs to Boston and the Wash.

Out in the country, some 1½ miles from Brayford Pool, or reached down a lane from the A57, is the isolated *Pyewipe* inn (the word means peewit or lapwing) beside the canal at ref: 948724. The original small, white-painted boatman's pub has had a restaurant added, but simplicity has not been spoiled. Take your drink outside to the towpath wall and watch the embanked Fossdyke unrolling its ribbon of water, the peewits still feeding in the wide, flat fields and, away on Lincoln's hill, the towers of the great cathedral seeking the sky. It will, I think, be a good moment.

51

Cromford
Map 119, ref: 300570

To visit Cromford is to find a lovely corner of Derbyshire: add a canal terminal associated with a creator of the industrial revolution, a fine aqueduct and steam pumping plant, and a spectacular inclined plane on a canal-connected railway, and this can be a memorable visit.

Richard Arkwright came to Cromford in 1771 and built cotton mills. In 1788 he supported the construction of the new Cromford Canal upwards from the Erewash Canal (a branch of the Trent). It was opened in 1794 with William Jessop as engineer. Though there is no longer a through connection, the top 5½ miles of canal from Cromford downwards are in the care of the Derbyshire County Council as an amenity.

I suggest a three-mile walk beginning at Cromford wharf, where once coal, building stone and raw materials for the mills arrived, and textiles and locally mined lead were shipped back. The wharf, yard and buildings still keep something of the atmosphere of working days. Then walk along the quiet towpath for about a mile of beautiful country past a swing bridge and High Peak wharf (to which we shall return) to Leawood pumping station. This was built in 1849 to raise water to the canal from the Derwent, supplies being fed by a tunnel into the basement of the pumphouse. Stone-built, it has a tall, wide-topped chimney, and houses a steam single-acting beam engine with a beam nearly 33ft long. The Cromford Canal Society are restoring it and arranging public steamings (enquiries: Dethick 345).

Continue a little further along the towpath to the aqueduct carrying the canal over the Derwent. With three arches, the centre one of 80ft span, 200yds long and 30ft high, it is workmanlike and impressive without being grand. Just beyond, the former Lea Wood branch, now dry, ran for $\frac{1}{4}$ mile to serve works at Lea. Then cross the canal by the footbridge and return to High Peak wharf.

During the Canal Age our ancestors wanted to shorten the London–Manchester route by building a High Peak canal between Cromford and Whaley Bridge (see No 36). A canal proved impracticable, but in 1831 the 33-mile Cromford & High Peak Railway joined the gap over a summit that rose to 1,264ft. A short extension in 1853 past High Peak wharf gave the line a link to the main London railway. The C & HP had nine inclined planes up and down which trucks had to be hauled by stationary steam engines, the stretches between being worked first by horses, later by locomotives. The last stretches, including the line down to High Peak junction, did not close till 1967.

At High Peak wharf, boat and railway cargoes could be exchanged at the shed that still throws its awning over the canal. The company's workshops were here, and remaining buildings include a locomotive servicing shed (to become an information centre) which has an inspection pit laid with original 4ft fish-bellied rails lettered 'C & H P Railway', and a row of railway workers' cottages. The first inclined plane, Sheep Pasture, leads off the wharf, past a water tank. Originally two separately worked planes with rises of 204ft and 261ft, in 1857 they were combined and worked as one incline 1,320yds long with a gradient varying between 1 in 8 and 1 in 9. A driving pulley at the top turned another at the bottom; round these ran a wire rope, to which trucks were attached by chains, ascending wagons being balanced by others descending.

Those who can walk up through the woods to the top will find a fine view of Cromford and the course of the canal down the Derwent valley. The stone-built engineless house stands there still. Further, however, at the top of the next (Middleton) incline, ref. 275552, the enginehouse still has an 1830 beam engine (enquiries Wirksworth 3204). If energy or age does not take you far up the incline, you can return to Cromford by a lane that runs beneath it.

52

Shardlow
Map 129, ref: 442303

Shardlow is a village that was largely created by the Trent & Mersey Canal, completed throughout in 1777. A mile up from the point at which the canal joins the navigable Trent at Derwent Mouth, through one broad lock, the place is also on the river and had a warehouse here before the canal was built. Shardlow was both a transhipment point between Trent craft working down to the tideway and narrow boats moving into the canal system, and a place where goods for Derby were transferred to road waggons.

Some old buildings have gone, many others have been converted. But very much remains, and now that the old canal port is a conservation area, its future is more assured. I am indebted to Mr Michael D. Mitchell and the Trent & Mersey Canal Society for the following survey and plan: it enables us to walk round the village and understand its structure.

1 This building is now a private house (probably nineteenth century), but was once the *Canal Tavern* mentioned in L.T.C. Rolt's *Narrow Boat*. It had its own slaughterhouse and bakery. The house marks the site of the only river warehouse (known to exist in 1766) before the canal port was built.

2 Lock 2 – much repaired.

3 Lockhouse, original in part.

4 The Clock Warehouse built in 1780. Note how this building once straddled a canal arm so that boats could be moored beneath for the

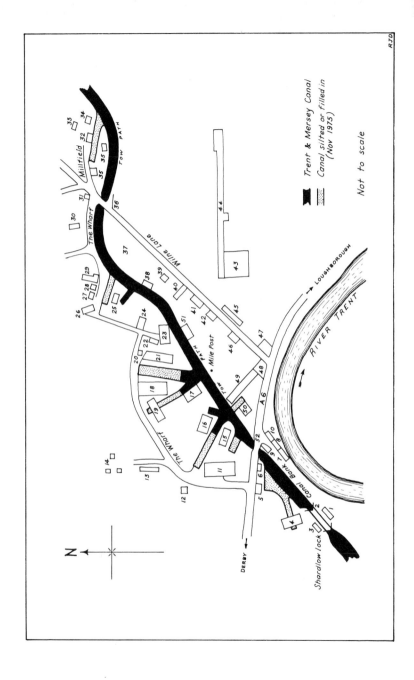

N

Millfield

TOW PATH

35 34
32
35
35
31
30
The Wharf
36
Wine Lane
37
26
27 28 29
25
24
23
22
21
20
18
17
19
16
15
The Wharf
14
13
12
11
5 6
Canal Bank
Shardlow lock
3
4
1
2
PATH
TOW PATH
Mile Post
39
38
40
41
42
51
46
45
47
48
49
50
52
10
8
9
7
A 6
43
44

DERBY

LOUGHBOROUGH

RIVER TRENT

Trent & Mersey Canal

Canal silted or filled in
(Nov 1975)

Not to scale

RJD

goods to be lifted up to be stored.

5   Originally a salt warehouse. It dates at least from 1778, and may be the port's oldest building.

6   Site of smithy, demolished about the time of World War I.

7   Modern house on site of old cottages.

8   ⎱ Original salt warehouses, now private houses and shop – note the
9   ⎰ bricked-up loading doorways.

10   An original port building. Previously a canal tavern, the *Holden Arms*, it is now a private house.

11   Canal workers' houses built before 1852. Slight alterations have been made.

12   Derwent House built 1794.

13   Typical canal cottages – original buildings.

14   New houses.

15   ⎱ Warehouses built about 1815.
16   ⎰

17   ⎱ Sites of post-1850 buildings now removed.
18   ⎰

19   Warehouse built 1792. Like No 4 this also straddled a canal arm, but the arches are now blocked up.

20   Original cottages.

21   Warehouse for iron, 1792. Became a soapworks by the 1900s.

22   The tall section was the *Ship* inn, the remainder cottages. The front of the former *Ship* now faces recent wooden buildings that stand on the site of Soresby's wharf.

23   Site of Soresby's wharf – what must have been a small brick ticket office remains – it can be seen from the towpath.

24   The Firs – a private house built before 1791.

25   Warehouse – note the windows. The boat repair yard occupied the land between this warehouse and the road, the now filled-in arm being in fact a slipway.

26   Original cottage and Wesleyan Methodist chapel (1859).

27   Trent Villa built in 1882. The initials TH stand for Tom Henshall, a well known local man.

28   The Wharf House (1799).

29   The *Malt Shovel* inn (this was a malt house together with the manager's house) built 1799. Note the gable end.

30   The *New Inn*, an original beer house.

31   This building, No 65a The Wharf, used to be the bakehouse.

32   No 1 Millfield – the former gatehouse to the corn mill.

33   Originally a four-storey granary. After a fire it was reduced to two storeys and made into two houses (Nos 3 and 5). Note the same type of gable end as at the *Malt Shovel*.

34   Original mill, now a house.

35   Houses, assumed to be built after the main port development.

36 The site of an original canal humped bridge.
37 Site of Trent Brewery (1790 and later extensions). The canalside site was Cowlishaw's wharf.
38 Cowlishaw's wharf.
39 The Lawn, the brewery manager's house, built 1795.
40 Original stables.
41 Original cottages.
42 Original stables or cottages.
43 Rope factory – original. Note the semicircular windows. It was closed about 1900.
44 Rope walk – connected with factory.
45 Later houses.
46 *The Lady in Grey*, now a public house, formerly the private house of the Soresby boating family, built pre-1790.
47 The *Navigation* inn – built as a private house.
48 Broughton House, built by the local Sutton family. Its garden was the other side of the *Navigation* inn.
49 ⎫ Original warehouses – note windows similar to those in the rope
50 ⎭ factory and warehouse by the boatyard. At one time these housed bottling plant and a bottle store for the brewery, the beer being brought round by water on pontoons.
51 Original stables.
52 This modern bridge stands near the site of 'Lazy' or 'Idle' bridge, so called because port workers would while away their time on it waiting for boats to arrive.

53

Foxton
Map 141, ref: 692895

Apart from the beauty of the place. there are two reasons for seeking out Foxton: the two extraordinary staircases of five narrow locks each, and the remains of the boat carrying inclined plane that worked early in the present century.

In 1793 a broad canal was begun from Leicester to the Nene at Northampton: by 1809 it had struggled past Foxton village to Market Harborough. There it stayed. A badly needed link between the Leicester canals leading to the Trent with its neighbouring coalfields and the Grand Junction (later the *new* Grand Union) Canal was provided in 1814 when the *old* Grand Union was built from Foxton 75ft up ten locks, along a winding summit level, and down seven locks at Watford to join the Grand Junction at Norton junction by Long Buckby.

Until the railways came the canal was a busy coal carrier. Then trade faded away. To get it back the Grand Junction, who had bought the Grand Union company, wanted to use barges carrying 70 tons instead of narrow boats. Instead of widening the locks, they decided to by-pass them with an inclined plane (see also No 25), which would speed up transit and save water.

A sloping concrete ramp was built on which rails were laid. Twin caissons ran sideways on these, each having eight wheels on four sets of rails, and able to carry one barge or two narrow boats. The caissons were linked by a steel cable passing round a hauling drum at the top of the incline. This was powered partly by counterbalance, partly by steam in an enginehouse at the top. The incline was designed by Gordon Thomas, the canal company's engineer, and opened in 1900. Results were not encouraging: it was clear that the coal trade would not return, and operating costs were too high in relation to actual traffic. The idea of a second incline at Watford was abandoned, and in 1911 Foxton incline ceased to be used, traffic again passing by the locks. It was dismantled in the 1920s.

From the Foxton-Gumley road (car-park and picnic area) one can walk to the top of the locks, with its lockhouse and magnificent view down the flight and away. On the way there, one can see to the right the silted-up approach canal to the top of the incline. The lock flight is in two staircases with a short passing pound between, each lock having its side-pond or individual reservoir. At the bottom, the canal passes under a bridge (refreshments, souvenirs, nearby) to a junction with the Leicester–Market Harborough line. Boat trips run from here (enquiries Kibworth 2285). Just to the right of the junction is the arm leading to the bottom of the incline. At the end are the remains of the two docks into which the caissons ran for the boats to be floated in and out. The ramp is overgrown, but some rail grooves can be made out. At the top, a wall of the enginehouse stands beside the upper approach canal. Altogether, an interesting day's sight, usually made jollier by watching some perplexed boat captain struggling with the instructions for working the staircases. It could have been me.

54

Newbold-on-Avon
Map 140, ref: 489773

Newbold is on the Avon, certainly, but to us it is on the Oxford Canal near Rugby: it has two tunnels and two pubs, and enables me to introduce the Oxford Canal curves.

This part of the Oxford Canal was laid out by Brindley and built in the 1770s. He tended to build canals which closely followed the contours, so maintaining the same height over considerable distances without embankments, cuttings or many locks, but at the cost of much winding. So building costs were kept down in days when extra time taken by boats did not matter much. By the 1820s, however, time meant much more money, so William Cubitt and the Oxford's company's engineer Frederick Wood straightened the northern part of the Oxford to just below Braunston between 1829 and 1834, cutting off no less than 13½ miles. And so, as we explore the northern Oxford, we often see graceful iron bridges, all made by the Horseley company of Tipton. They carry the straightened towpath over old cuts, some derelict and weedy, some used for short distances for boatyards and moorings. Those few who explore the old curves are rewarded with here and there an old bridge, aqueduct, wharf or tunnel.

So at Newbold. If from the B4112 we get onto the towpath past the *Boat* and the *Barley Mow*, both beside the wharf, and walk north, we shall come to the newer Newbold tunnel of 1834, 350yds long, wide enough for narrow boats to pass, designed for towpaths on each side. But if we now go back past the pubs, up the road a little way, into the churchyard, and out by a gate at the far right-hand corner, we shall come to the bed of an old curve. Turn right, and there is the entrance to the original narrow Newbold tunnel, 125yds long, towline marks still showing on the entrance brickwork. The tunnel runs under the churchyard and the road, the old curve then passing by the two pubs to join the present route. The OS map shows the line of the curve in the opposite direction, meandering round to the west and north to join the straightened line again at ref: 482778, just west of the bridge that carries the B4112 over the canal.

Places Nearby
From Newbold, make for the bridge that takes the A427 over the canal at ref: 440807, and seek the towpath on the north-western side. Here the new canal lies straight ahead past the wharf built after straightening, and the old one curves sharply to the right under a railway bridge and on to Stretton old wharf, now a hire cruiser base. If we now turn and walk back under the A427 bridge, we shall come out on an embankment over the valley of the Smite brook, beyond which the original canal swung to the right into the village of Brinklow. But the embankment is not all it seems. To the left as we walk over it, it is indeed an embankment except for a single arch for the Smite brook, but to the right, if one scrambles down into a lake of dried dredgings (choose dry weather for this one) one can look up at great brick arches, crumbling at the edges. They are the remains of what is, I suppose, Brindley's biggest aqueduct in terms of height combined with length. He designed this considerable structure for the original canal, with twelve arches each of 22ft span, the whole being some 300ft long and 31ft 6in high at the highest point. It could, however, only take narrow boats in single file and so, when the canal was straightened, this bottleneck was removed, not by demolishing it and substituting an embankment – that would have interrupted traffic – but by building an embankment alongside, and then removing one side. The Smite brook runs under one of the original arches, though widened to full width. Brinklow Arches are worth seeing, and are little known.

55

Braunston
Map 152, ref: 538658

Braunston, at the junction of the old Grand Junction and the Oxford Canals not far from Rugby, epitomises canal history. For thereabouts are, if you like, the seven ages of canals set out for all to see, from Wolfhamcote tunnel built in Brindley's day to the restaurant of the canalside *Rose and Castle*.

Let me first explain how canals came to Braunston. The narrow-boat Oxford Canal is the oldest. Begun in 1768, it had by 1774 wound its way from the Coventry Canal south past Braunston as far as Napton. But in those days the canal line came in from the north, turned towards Braunston at the present junction, and then under the iron bridge and into what is now the Ladyline yard, and by a winding course (traceable on the OS map) up one side of the river Leam, across, down the other, and then through Wolfhamcote to rejoin the present canal line on to Napton. In 1793 a new canal, the Grand Junction, was authorised as a barge or broad line from Brentford (No 4) to Braunston. Completed in 1805, it arrived through Braunston tunnel and down six locks to join the Oxford by the Ladyline bridge. Finally, between 1829 and 1834 the Oxford company shortened their winding line: a new canal was then made from just west of Braunston direct to near Wolfhamcote, so eliminating the old loop. Meanwhile, the Grand Junction had provided steam plant at the foot of the locks to pump water from three small inter-connected reservoirs beside the bottom lock, into which lockage water was led, back to the top of the flight.

Arriving at Braunston by the A45 (see plan on p148 of Alan Faulkner's book), let us gain the towpath and walk east towards the locks. On the right is the old red-brick toll-office at the end of the Grand Junction Canal (a lock here was removed in the 1930s), and then, sharp right, the old line of the Oxford running into the Ladyline marina; half right, too, through the marina, a short branch that led to the Daventry road. The graceful iron bridge from the Horseley Ironworks dates from the 1830s. Before the marina came, this site was used by narrow-boat building and carrying companies, and a crane and some buildings from the time of the last of them, Nurser's, still remain. Beyond are the reservoirs, used also as moorings, from which water is still pumped back, and then the enginehouse where now an electric pump does the work. On the left, canal buildings and a dry-dock are used by a pleasure craft boatyard.

Beside the third lock is the *Nelson* inn, formerly a good pull-up for working boatmen, now for those in cruisers. A short way beyond the top lock is the feeder from the pumping back at Braunston below, and then the entrance to the tunnel, $1\frac{1}{8}$ miles long, opened in 1796. When cruising through it, one finds a mild S-bend in the middle, the mistake of a resident engineer not watching the contractor. A horse path over the top will take the energetic to the other end.

In the opposite direction along the towpath from where we started, the astonishing architecture of the *Rose and Castle* lies across the canal. Beyond is the junction. To the left, first in a cutting, then on an embankment called Braunston Puddle Banks, the Oxford's later line leads to Oxford and also via Napton to Birmingham; to the right the Oxford's old line leads towards Coventry. Just before the junction, across from the towpath, can be seen the masonry beginnings of what was planned in the 1930s as a big transhipment basin.

To visit the tiny and very odd little tunnel at Wolfhamcote (map 151, ref: 526653) on the disused loop, you can take a track direct from Braunston, or a longer road via Willoughby and Sawbridge. The tunnel is worth seeing if only to wonder why, with so little above and only 33yds long, it was built at all, and why wide when the Oxford is a narrow canal.

56

The Waterways Museum, Stoke Bruerne
(Map 152, ref: 743499)

At the village of Stoke Bruerne in Northamptonshire, not far

from the M1 and A5, Towcester or Northampton, is the canal-side Waterways Museum, which draws over 100,000 visitors a year to its collection of canalia, and to watch cruisers working through the lock, stroll up to the portal of Blisworth tunnel, or have a drink or a game of Northamptonshire skittles (the oval cheeses are thrown with tremendous thumps) in the thatched *Boat Inn*.

William Jessop, engineer of the Grand Junction Canal, the broad modern canal line that was to link the Midlands with London and make obsolete the older inefficient route by way of Oxford and the Thames, had trouble with springs of water in his first attempt to cut Blisworth tunnel. So, while he tried again, a horse tramroad was built from Blisworth village over the hill down past Stoke Bruerne, to end below the present locks. Traffic passed on this until, in 1805, the second tunnel was finished and the flight of seven wide locks up to the village from the south completed.

I like to approach Stoke Bruerne from the tunnel, by boat or down the towpath. The canal widens: on the left is the three-storey museum with its attendant shop; beyond are stone houses and then a charming one in brick, once a shop, later a post office, now a refreshment room and the home of the museum's curator. To the right is a wharf cottage, once a wharfinger's house, another shop, former stables now used as a tearoom, and then the *Boat*. Ahead, the working lock is to the left, first of a flight falling under the white painted bridge. To its right, a disused fellow lock (the older one, that in present use having been built later) now houses a huge boat-weighing machine complete with narrow boat in the livery of Fellows, Morton & Clayton, once-famous canal carriers. These outsize scales (this one dates from 1834 and came from the Glamorganshire Canal at Cardiff) were used to weigh boats and their cargoes whenever toll-collectors thought craft were carrying more than the waybills showed.

A line of cruisers borders the canal bank, while behind the locks the poplars rise, a backdrop to as pretty a waterways scene as any in Britain. Here at Stoke Bruerne one can see a lot of people enjoying themselves alongside or on a canal – and a pleasant sight it is.

The museum was begun on the initiative of John James, a retired Stoke Bruerne lockkeeper and perennial character, and of Sir Reginald Kerr, Waterways Manager of the British Transport Commission; it was housed in a disused steam mill and opened in 1963. Now it occupies all three floors of its building. Here is a narrow-boat cabin as it once was; working boat engines, traditional clothes for people and horses, models, prints, pictures, maps, signs, notices, painted water cans, Measham teapots, company badges and buttons, and much else. I enjoy it just as much every time I go back. The Waterways Museum is open nearly all the year round (enquiries Northampton 862229). There is a free museum car park, and short boat trips to the tunnel.

Places Nearby
Northwards, it is only a few hundred yards to the portals of Blisworth tunnel, almost $1\frac{3}{4}$ miles long. There are two little buildings by the tunnel entrance; one was a horse stable, the other a workshop for maintaining the former tunnel tugs. A pleasant walk leads off the towpath and takes you by the old horse track

over the top. You will have glimpses of the tunnel ventilator shafts and, if you are a keen-eyed industrial archaeologist, of the old horse tramroad track, before reaching Blisworth village and the tunnel's other end in a deep wooded cutting. A red-brick canal warehouse, dated 1879, stands by the water.

Southwards, a pleasant walk takes you down the locks. At the bottom the river Tove comes in from the east to unite with the canal for $\frac{3}{4}$ mile before leaving it again for the west, short of quiet Grafton Regis.

57

Denver Sluice
Map 143, ref: 587009

Sir Cornelius Vermuyden, engaged by the Duke of Bedford to drain a great flooded area of the Fens, assisted by Col William Dodson, first built a sluice at Denver in 1652.

He began by cutting a new channel, the Old Bedford River, from Denver to Earith much higher up the Ouse, to relieve the old and winding course of the river past Ely. A parallel drain, the New Bedford or Hundred Foot, followed. Then Denver Sluice itself, across the Ouse just upstream of the entrance to the New Bedford. By closing the sluice on a rising tide up the Ouse from King's Lynn, he proposed to stop the tide flooding into the fenlands, and turn it instead up the embanked Hundred Foot until it had lost its power; by opening it on the ebb, to lower the river level and so drain the lands on each side of it. He was right, but no-one then realised that, as the water drained out, so the peatland would shrink, causing the land surface to sink below the rivers and cease draining into them. And so, after some forty years, wind pumps turning scoopwheels began to spread through fenland to pump water out of the land drains up into the rivers. From 1817 steam pumps were added and from the mid-nineteenth century centrifugal pumps superseded scoopwheels. Now, diesel or electric pumps do the work. A steam engine and scoopwheel are preserved at Stretham (No 58). The result of all this is

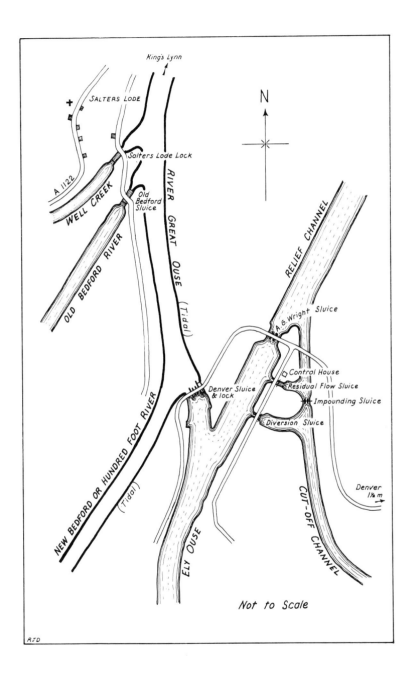

that Fenland rivers run above the land, and are themselves embanked.

Vermuyden's original Denver sluice was rebuilt in 1682, but collapsed in 1715. Labelye rebuilt it in 1751, but its existence caused endless friction between drainage interests and those who used the river for transport. On the whole, drainage won. The present sluice was designed by Sir John Rennie and erected in 1834. Visible for miles across the flat lands, it incorporates a huge vertically-rising gate, three sets of sluices, and a lock with two sets of gates, enabling it to work in either direction according to water level.

Denver is only one of five sets of water controls in the neighbourhood. The two most modern can be seen on the way to Denver Sluice from the A10. After the great Fenland floods of 1947, a large new drain, the Relief Channel, was cut from the Ouse just above King's Lynn, where tail-sluices were installed, running parallel and to the east of the river to join it again above Denver Sluice. From this another channel, the Cut-off, swings away to the east and then south to end in the river Lark near Mildenhall. The Relief Channel has the great three-gated A.G. Wright sluice at Denver, the Cut-off channel its own impounding sluice, with two others connecting the Cut-off channel to the Ely Ouse.

Having seen them and Denver Sluice itself, it would be wise to call at the *Jenyns Arms*, its face to the Ely Ouse just above the sluice, its back to the New Bedford River. Once it was a lodging place for the berthsmen who piloted craft downwards along the Ouse's tricky tideway to King's Lynn. Cruiser crews call here now – and others who, like ourselves, have come to see Denver's works of man.

Oddly, there is no footpath bridge here over the New Bedford River that would enable us to walk easily to examine the other two interesting channels that enter the Ouse just below, though they can be seen across the river from the embankment below the sluice. Instead, one must drive to Denver village, into Downham, turn left and out again on the A1122 to Salter's Lode, taking a left-hand turn by the post office.

One comes first to Salter's Lode lock. Through this a boat

can enter Well Creek from the tideway, and so get access to the Middle Levels, the network of navigable drains through which – and their fishermen – one can find one's way to Peterborough and the Nene. The lock has an electrically operated guillotine gate at the tidal end, and three pairs of mitre-gates.

A little further along the lane is the Old Bedford sluice at the bottom of the Old Bedford River, as odd a contraption as one will see anywhere. It has two pairs of gates, high on the tidal side, low on that of the drain, the first pair forming a seal with the bridge that stands between them. The pairs of gates are connected by chains; as one pair opens with the tide, the other shuts. Boats can only pass through this sluice for up to twenty minutes once a day on the ebb, when both pairs of gates can be opened together. First the small gates are opened, then the big ones winched back to give a passage.

And so, perhaps, to King's Lynn or Ely to round off your waterside day.

58

Cambridge
Map 154

The Cambridge 'Backs', perhaps the most beautiful stretch of navigable water in England, a glimpse of a Roman canal, a surviving Fenland steam pumping engine, and locks with gates facing both ways: all make a memorable group of sights to see.

The Cam ceases to be navigable in King's Mill pond on the far side of Silver Street bridge. From here down to Magdalene bridge, the Backs, past six colleges, is a most lovely stretch of old buildings, lawns, willows, sunlight and shadow, bird song, ducks, punts and college bridges. In medieval times, when Cambridge was a busy port for goods brought up the Great Ouse and Cam from Kings Lynn, wharves stretched over the land where now college gardens run. After the colleges had been built, there was still traffic up to King's Mill, the towing horses later using a towpath built in the river: old prints show them half-submerged.

Baits Bite lock on the Cam, with its swan-necked lock-beams

Below Magdalene bridge is the Common Hithe (or wharf) at Quayside, some 400yds above Jesus lock, the normal highest point for powered craft, still with pubs with names from commercial days (the last working boat left in 1932). The stretch of river from the *Pike and Eel* down to Baits Bite lock, $3\frac{1}{2}$ miles below Jesus lock, is used for college and university rowing, an interesting sight during term.

Places Nearby
Baits Bite lock (ref: 486620) is a delight. Prettily sited, it is reached down a lane from Milton and along the halingway, an old term still used on a notice. It has swan-necked lock-beams and a very elementary swing bridge over the centre of the lock, instead of walkways on the lock gates.

From Baits Bite I suggest you seek the Caerdyke, the Roman waterway 73 miles long that began at Waterbeach on the Cam and ran to the Witham near Lincoln (No 50) to join the Fossdyke. This now forms the drainage ditch on the south-west side of Waterbeach airfield, alongside the A10 between refs: 488660 and

481671. From the latter point the line can be seen heading NNW across the fields. A more primitive stretch can be found on a minor road at 477689.

Beside the Great Ouse at ref: 515729, reached from a lane called Green End in Stretham village, we can find Stretham Old Engine. Now preserved and open to visitors throughout the year, it dates from 1831, the earliest and largest remaining steam-powered drainage pumping engine in the Fens. It is housed in a tripartite building, visible long before you reach it, comprising a one-storey boilerhouse and chimney, a large and tall engine-house, and a smaller scoopwheel building. The 60hp beam engine with its 24ft diameter flywheel turned a 37ft diameter scoopwheel that raised the water. Everything is still there and can be seen.

Off the Cam run the lodes. These are navigable land drains, their inner ends below ground level, their river junctions well above it. When floods come, the locks at the lode junctions are closed to stop river water entering, and pumps then lift land water from the lodes up into the river to be carried away. Formerly, the lodes carried commercial traffic to the villages at their heads.

For a quick visit, see Upware lock (ref: 537698) that gives access to Reach lode and its branches, Burwell and Wicken lodes. Upware lock has an electrically powered guillotine upper gate and duplicated lower gates. Near the head of Wicken lode is the National Trust's nature reserve, Wicken Fen. End at the little port of Commercial End (ref: 556630) at the head of Swaffham Bulbeck lode. There are warehouses, one dated 1662, and the delightful Merchant's House. In the 1790s, corn was shipped from here for Kings Lynn, and coal brought back.

59

Flatford Lock
Map 168, ref: 076333

We have all seen a Constable painting of the Suffolk Stour navigation of his time, with its bluff-bowed clinker-built lighters, and locks with overhead galley-beams. Indeed, the painter's father was one of the Stour Commissioners. Sadly the Stour, winding through the lovely country of the Essex-Suffolk border, is now only navigable in short stretches, though a local Trust is working to change that. At Flatford, however, a lock has been restored: it was opened in 1975.

Stour locks once had lock gates which did not, as is normal, incorporate heelposts on the inner sides which rotated in semi-circular quoins cut in the masonry of the lockside, and were held upright by iron straps. Instead, like ordinary field-gates, the lock gates worked on hooks and rides. Their weight, however, tended to pull them together, and so overhead galley-beams were provided to hold the gate-posts upright. Paddles are worked one notch at a time with a handspike, as on the Calder & Hebble.

Apart from the locks, the Stour used to have two other navigational oddities. Instead of towpath gates, low stiles marked land boundaries, and towing horses were trained to jump these, in the prancing fashion we can see in the painter's *The Leaping Horse*. Again, when the towpath changed sides on most naviga-tions, either a bridge or a ferry-boat was provided to carry the horses over. Not, however, on the Stour. Instead, small wooden piers were built nearly opposite to each other at crossings, from which horses were taught to jump on to a lighter's foredeck, be carried over, and then jump off again. Stour towing horses must have got very tired of all that jumping, for one voyage from Sudbury to Manningtree involved 123 jumps and 20 crossings.

Approach picturesque Flatford by the (one way) lane from East Bergholt church (map 155): you will find a car park. The lock, set in trees, is over the timber bridge and to the left. Nearby, but not open to the public, is Flatford mill, owned by the National-al Trust and leased to the Field Studies Council. As picturesque a building as one could expect from one of England's loveliest rivers, the mill dates from the fifteenth century. It was once owned by Constable's father, and the painter worked there for a year. Willy Lott's Cottage, early seventeenth century, just beyond the mill, appears in *The Hay Wain*.

At the sixteenth century Thatched Cottage one can have tea, or hire a rowing boat. If you want to pass the lock, ask for a key and bar (deposit payable). Or why not row up to Dedham, full of good buildings, including the church, two medieval pubs and Constable's grammar school? Above the B1029 bridge (ref: 056336) is a path between the water and Dedham mill, leading to the lock and brick lock cottage with its pointed windows. Further up the road, in Dedham, a footpath leads to the charming Countryside Centre backing onto a pretty playing field. An exhibit here by the River Stour Trust explains the navigation story.

Higher up the river is Stratford St Mary. Between the *Black Horse* (try the ploughman's lunch) and the *Swan*, a path leads over sluices. Just past them, turn right along a path between channels (the river to your right, the old navigation cut to your left) for 200 yds to unrestored Stratford lock.

60

Heybridge Basin and Maldon
Map 168, ref: 872068

At Heybridge Basin by Maldon in Essex, the Chelmer & Blackwater Navigation, opened in 1797, reaches the tides after its fourteen-mile journey from Chelmsford. John Rennie made it in three sections: as a canalisation of the Chelmer from Chelmsford to Beeleigh; then of the Blackwater; and lastly as a true canal from near Maldon to Heybridge. The basin there, with a tidal lock into the Blackwater estuary, was intended for sailing ships: there they could tranship their cargoes of timber, coal and provisions to broad, shallow-draught 25-ton barges for Chelmsford. Timber barges survived until a few years ago.

A nice two-storey bow-windowed lockhouse flanks the entrance lock on one side, a row of cottages, pink, white and grey, some weatherboarded, and the *Old Ship* in dark red wash the other. Round the corner is the *Jolly Sailor*. Justly, this charming group of buildings now forms part of a conservation area. The lower gate of the tide-lock is of an unusual type: of caisson construction, it slides sideways, electrically powered and chain-

Maldon: 'A huddle of interesting craft, including several sailing barges and two old steam tugs'

operated. As I stood at the lock, the channel to the sea ran to the left, that to Maldon to the right. Straight ahead is Northey island, parting the Blackwater into two. The estuary was full of sails. In the basin and along the canal some 180 boats of all shapes and sizes were moored, including three sailing barges and one or two Dutchmen.

From the basin I suggest a walk up the towpath past the only canal-served cemetery I know to a waterway oddity, a canal level-crossing, at ref: 840084. First comes Beeleigh flood-lock, its balance beams steeply up-slanting, lying beneath a bridge. Now the Blackwater swings away to the right, while the navigation runs left across the top of the flood weir that maintains the level of the canalised section, paralleled by the wooden towpath bridge. Beneath, the Blackwater's overflow water rushes to join the Chelmer, here only two hundred yards away. Beyond the level crossing, Beeleigh lock lifts the navigation to the level at which, not far ahead, it will enter the Chelmer and follow it to

Chelmsford. Beeleigh lock is as pleasant a place to sit on a summer's day as one could find. On one side greensward, if you could so call a sheet of buttercups and daisies, on the other trees, all around the running of water. A footpath from the lock leads across a fine collection of weirs to a lane that takes one to Maldon. The level crossing can be approached by car down the lane past Beeleigh Grange, but the last few hundred yards must be walked.

Maldon is picturesque and comfortable, and down by the water becomes a seaboots-and-jersey kind of place. Masts are everywhere. Down North Street to the Hythe are sailmakers, riggers and yacht chandlers. The *Queen's Head* backs onto the water. Beyond is a huddle of interesting craft, including several sailing barges – some can be chartered – and two old steam tugs. Upstream, the coaster *Bill Brush* may be in at Fulbridge wharf, opposite the offices of A.J. Brush Ltd, which have over the door the date 1924 and, delightfully, a shrimp cut in brick.

In July the Blackwater Sailing Barge Match takes place at Maldon. Membership of the Match is cheap, and enables you to reserve seats on following craft, attend the crews' supper, and take part in social activities.

Where to Find more Information

The numbers in the list below correspond with those of the sights in the text.

For general information use the six Nicholson's *Guides* to the Thames and to the waterways of the South East, South West, North East, North West and Midlands, the last-named to some extent overlapping the previous four.

For history, consult the 'Canals of the British Isles' (CBI) series published by David & Charles. Full titles are as follows and each is followed by the abbreviation used in the list:

Charles Hadfield *The Canals of South and South East England (CSSEE)*
Charles Hadfield *The Canals of South West England (CSWE)*
Charles Hadfield *The Canals of the West Midlands (CWM)*
Charles Hadfield *The Canals of the East Midlands (CEM)*
Charles Hadfield *The Canals of South Wales and the Border (CSWB)*
Charles Hadfield *The Canals of Yorkshire and North East England (CYNEE)*

Charles Hadfield and Gordon Biddle *The Canals of North West England* (*CNWE*)

Charles Hadfield and John Norris *Waterways to Stratford* (*WS*)

Jean Lindsay *The Canals of Scotland* (*CS*)

John Boyes and Ronald Russell *The Canals of Eastern England* (*CEE*)

(The last-named title should be published in 1977. All the others are published.)

Other useful general books are:

Ronald Russell *Lost Canals of England and Wales* (David & Charles), a book about canals that are no longer used.

P. J. G. Ransom *Waterways Restored* (Faber), covering all waterway restoration schemes.

Ronald Russell *Waterside Pubs* (David & Charles)

Hugh McKnight *The Shell Book of Inland Waterways* (David & Charles), full of interesting articles and with a good gazetteer.

These can be bought in any bookshop, or from the Inland Waterways Association, 114 Regent's Park Road, London NW1 8UQ. The sights I have described are also covered in more detail by many local pamphlets and booklets, too quickly changing to be usefully listed. Most can be bought on the spot: most also are available from the Inland Waterways Association. Send for a book and booklet list.

For more information about a 'sight', consult the following:

1 Nicholson, *South east*; CBI, *CEM*; A. H. Faulkner, *The Grand Junction Canal* (David & Charles); London street atlas.

2 Nicholson, *South east, Thames*; CBI, *CEE* and *CEM*; London street atlas.

3 Nicholson, *Thames*; F. S. Thacker, *The Thames Highway: Locks and Weirs* (David & Charles reprint); London street atlas.

4 Nicholson, *South east, Thames*; CBI, *CEM*; A. H. Faulkner, *The Grand Junction Canal* (David & Charles), historical plan p210; F. S. Thacker, *The Thames Highway: Locks and Weirs* (David & Charles reprint); London street atlas.

5 CBI, *CSSEE*; P. A. L. Vine, *The Royal Military Canal* (David & Charles).

6 CBI, *CSSEE*; P. A. L. Vine, *London's Lost Route to the Sea* (David & Charles).

7 Nicholson, *South east*; CBI, *CEM*; A. H. Faulkner, *The Grand Junction Canal* (David & Charles); *The Canal at Tring* (British Waterways Board); *Tring Reservoirs: National Nature Reserve* (Nature Conservancy).

8 Nicholson, *Thames*; CBI, *CSSEE*; L. J. Dalby, *The Wilts and Berks Canal* (Oakwood Press); F. S. Thacker, *The Thames Highway: Locks and Weirs* (David & Charles reprint).

9 Nicholson, *South west*; CBI, *CSSEE*; K. R. Clew, *The Kennet & Avon Canal* (David & Charles).

10 Nicholson, *South west*; CBI, *CSSEE*; K. R. Clew, *The Kennet & Avon Canal*.

11 CBI, *CSWE*; H. Harris, *The Grand Western Canal* (David & Charles).

12 CBI, *CSWE*.

13 CBI, *CSWE*; F. Booker, *Industrial Archaeology of the Tamar Valley* (David & Charles). Enquiries to Warden, Morwellham Quay Centre for Recreation and Education, Tavistock, Devon.

14 Nicholson, *South west*; CBI, *CSSEE*; *Sharpness: centenary of the new dock, 1874–1974* (British Waterways Board).

15 CBI, *CSSEE*; H. Household, *The Thames & Severn Canal* (David & Charles); *The Thames and Severn Canal* (Corinium Museum, Cirencester).

16 CBI, *CSWB*; R. A. Stevens, *Towpath Guide No 2: Brecknock & Abergavenny and Monmouthshire Canals* (Goose & Son).

17 Nicholson, *South west*; CBI, *CSWB*; R. A. Stevens, *Towpath Guide No 2: Brecknock & Abergavenny and Monmouthshire Canals* (Goose & Son).

18 Nicholson, *South west*; CBI, *CWM*; J. I. Langford, *Towpath Guide No 1: Staffordshire and Worcestershire Canal* (Goose & Son); C. W. F. Garrett, 'Bewdley and the Stinking Ditch: An Exposition', in *Essays towards a history of Bewdley*, ed. Snell (Bewdley Research Group).

19 Nicholson, *South west*; CBI, *CWM*.

20 Nicholson, *Midlands*; CBI, *CWM*; Birmingham street atlas; Enquiries about Black Country Museum to BCM Development Office, Fisher St, Dudley, West Midlands.

21 Nicholson, *Midlands*; CBI, *CWM*; S. R. Broadbridge, *The Birmingham Canal Navigations, 1768–1846* (David & Charles); Birmingham street atlas.

22 Nicholson, *Midlands*; CBI, *CWM*; S. R. Broadbridge, *The Birmingham Canal Navigations, 1768–1846* (David & Charles); Birmingham street atlas.

23 Nicholson, *South west*; CBI, *WS* and *CWM*.

24 Nicholson, *South west*; CBI, *WS*.

25 CBI, *CWM*; enquiries from Ironbridge Gorge Museum Trust, Church Hill, Ironbridge, Telford, Salop, TF8 7RE.

26 Nicholson, *North west*; CBI, *CWM*.

27 Nicholson, *North west*; CBI, *CWM*; P. J. G. Ransom, *Waterways Restored* (Faber).

28 Nicholson, *North west*; CBI, *CWM*; L. T. C. Rolt, *Thomas Telford* (Longmans).

29 Nicholson, *North west*; CBI, *CWM*; L. T. C. Rolt, *Thomas Telford* (Longmans).

30 (*Great Haywood*) Nicholson, *North west*; CBI, *CWM*; J. I. Langford,

Towpath Guide No 1: Staffordshire and Worcestershire Canal (Goose & Son); (*Fradley*) Nicholson, *North west*, *South east*; CBI, *CWM* and *CEM*; (*Huddlesford*) Nicholson, *South east*; CBI, *CEM*.

31 Nicholson, *North west*; CBI, *CWM*.
32 Nicholson, *North west*; CBI, *CWM*.
33 Nicholson, *North west*; CBI, *CWM*.
34 Nicholson, *North west*; CBI, *CNWE*.
35 CBI, *CNWE*; Manchester and District street atlas.
36 Nicholson, *North west*; CBI, *CNWE* (*Peak Forest Canal*) and *CWM* (*Macclesfield Canal*).
37 Nicholson, *North west*; CBI, *CNWE*.
38 Nicholson, *North west*; CBI, *CNWE*.
39 CBI, *CNWE*; 'The Carlisle Canal', History Resources Folder at Carlisle Museum.
40 CBI, *CS*.
41 CBI, *CS*; A. D. Cameron, *The Caledonian Canal* (Dalton).
42 CBI, *CS*.
43 Nicholson, *North east*; CBI, *CYNEE*.
44 CBI, *CYNEE*.
45 Nicholson, *North east*; CBI, *CYNEE*; B. F. Duckham, *The Yorkshire Ouse* (David & Charles).
46 Nicholson, *North west*; CBI, *CNWE*.
47 Nicholson, *North east*; CBI, *CYNEE* (*Calder & Hebble*) and *CNWE* (*Rochdale*).
48 Nicholson, *North east*; CBI, *CYNEE*.
49 Nicholson, *North east*; CBI, *CYNEE*; street plans of Doncaster and Sheffield.
50 Nicholson, *North east*; CBI, *CEE*.
51 CBI, *CEM* (*Cromford Canal*) and *CNWE* (*C & HPR*).
52 Nicholson, *North east*; CBI, *CWM*.
53 Nicholson, *South east*; CBI, *CEM;* P. A. Stevens, *The Leicester Line* (David & Charles).
54 Nicholson, *South east*; CBI, *CEM*.
55 Nicholson, *South east*; CBI, *CEM*; A. H. Faulkner, *The Grand Junction Canal* (David & Charles).
56 Nicholson, *South east*; CBI, *CEM*; A. H. Faulkner, *The Grand Junction Canal* (David & Charles); enquiries Waterways Museum, Stoke Bruerne, nr Towcester, Northants, NN12 7SE.
57 CBI, *CEE*; J. K. Wilson, *Fenland Barge Traffic* (Robert Wilson).
58 CBI, *CEE*; Cambridge street plan.
59 CBI, *CEE*.
60 CBI, *CEE*; Maldon guide book.

ACKNOWLEDGEMENTS

A very large number of people have helped me with this book – by answering enquiries, reading drafts, or lending me material. They will forgive me if I do not list their names, but I thank them very much for their generous assistance.

R. G. Cox has provided some delightful drawings, and R. J. Dean the maps and plans. I am grateful to the Ironbridge Gorge Museum Trust for permission to reproduce the drawing in No 25, to the British Waterways Board for the photographs in Nos 7, 28, 34, 36, 40, and 46, and for the cover transparencies, and to Derek Pratt for Nos 30 and 33.

Finally, my thanks go to my secretary, Mrs Dawn Bijl, who typed so many letters and drafts, Mrs Frances Pratt, who kindly read the proofs, and to my wife who, accompanying me on my voyages of discovery or rediscovery, has shown me much that otherwise I should have missed.

INDEX OF CANALS AND RIVER NAVIGATIONS

(Figures refer to 'sight' numbers, not to page numbers)

ACKNOWLEDGEMENTS

A very large number of people have helped me with this book – by answering enquiries, reading drafts, or lending me material. They will forgive me if I do not list their names, but I thank them very much for their generous assistance.

R. G. Cox has provided some delightful drawings, and R. J. Dean the maps and plans. I am grateful to the Ironbridge Gorge Museum Trust for permission to reproduce the drawing in No 25, to the British Waterways Board for the photographs in Nos 7, 28, 34, 36, 40, and 46, and for the cover transparencies, and to Derek Pratt for Nos 30 and 33.

Finally, my thanks go to my secretary, Mrs Dawn Bijl, who typed so many letters and drafts, Mrs Frances Pratt, who kindly read the proofs, and to my wife who, accompanying me on my voyages of discovery or rediscovery, has shown me much that otherwise I should have missed.

INDEX OF CANALS AND RIVER NAVIGATIONS

(Figures refer to 'sight' numbers, not to page numbers)